TERROR AND SUICIDE ATTACKS:
AN ISLAMIC PERSPECTIVE

CONTRIBUTORS

M. FETHULLAH GÜLEN – Islamic scholar and thinker and a prominent activist in interfaith dialogue and the promotion of education.

DR. IBRAHIM CANAN – Professor of Hadith at Marmara University, Istanbul. He translated more than 7,000 hadith into Turkish to make an eighteen-volume compilation of *al-Kutub al Sitta*.

DR. HAMZA AKTAN – Professor of Islamic Law at Atatürk University, Erzurum.

DR. BEKIR KARLIĞA – Professor of Islamic Philosophy at Marmara University, Istanbul.

ALI BULAÇ – Columnist for *Zaman* newspaper; a sociologist and theologian with more than thirty books on Islam and the Islamic world.

DR. NEVZAT TARHAN – Professor of Psychiatry and current director of "İDER – Human Values and Spiritual Health Foundation." He is the ex-director of "The Memory Center, Psychiatry Clinic" in Turkey.

DR. HIKMET YÜCEOĞLU – Professor emeritus of History of Sufism.

DR. ERGÜN ÇAPAN – PhD on Tafsir (Qur'anic commentary). He currently works for Akademik Araştırmalar Vakfı in Istanbul, and editor-in-chief of *Yeni Ümit*, a quarterly journal of Islamic sciences published in Turkey.

DR. AHMET GÜNEŞ – PhD on Islamic Law and currently teaching at Atatürk University, Erzurum.

DR. ADIL ÖKSÜZ – PhD on Islamic Law and currently teaching at Sakarya University, Adapazarı.

An Islamic Perspective

TERROR
and SUICIDE ATTACKS

Edited by Ergün Çapan

Light

New Jersey
2004

Published by The Light, Inc.
26 Worlds Fair Dr. Unit C
Somerset, New Jersey, 08873, USA
E-mail: contact@thelightinc.com
www.thelightpublishing.com

Translated by Nagihan Haliloğlu, Mükerrem Faniküçükmehmedoğlu
English text edited by Jane Louise Kandur, Hakan Yeşilova

Library of Congress PCN 2004110730

ISBN 1-932099-74-3

Printed by Mega Basım
Istanbul, Turkey

September 2004

TABLE OF CONTENTS

"In True Islam, Terror Does Not Exist."

M. Fethullah Gülen

Islam as the Religion of Peace and Tolerance

İbrahim Canan

Acts of Terror and Suicide Attacks
in the Light of the Qur'an and the Sunna

Hamza Aktan

Religion, Terror, War, and the Need for Global Ethics

Bekir Karlığa

Jihad

Ali Bulaç

Terror and Chemical Weapons Leading to Terror

Nevzat Tarhan

Martyrdom—A Definition
Can a Terrorist Be a Martyr?

Hikmet Yüceoğlu

Suicide Attacks and Islam

Ergün Çapan

Views on the Rules of War
in Islamic Law

Ahmet Güneş

Murder and Its Punishment in the Qur'an and the Torah

Adil Öksüz

PREFACE

In the world media, "Islam" and "terror" are frequently mentioned together; phrases such as "Muslim terrorists" have become commonplace. How appropriate is it to utter the words "Islam" and "terror" side by side? Is it even appropriate to mention any word that implies terrorism in juxtaposition with Islam? Do the fundamental sources of Islam and the traditions of various societies in different places throughout the history permit terrorism? Or is juxtaposing Islam and terrorism nothing but an attempt to tarnish the bright face of Islam; in fact, this is essentially what has happened. Does jihad—directly or indirectly—mean terror? What is the stance of Islam on suicide attacks, attacks about which it cannot be known where, when, or against whom they will be carried out, or who will be cruelly murdered?

We felt that in order to find satisfactory answers to these questions, and to similar other questions, and to communicate these answers to world public opinion, that it was a historical obligation to investigate these issues with experts in the relevant fields. Thus, we consulted the authorities from the relevant fields, as the most scientific and appropriate approach to learn about a subject is to learn from those who have expertise. In fact, just as it would not be sensible to seek the advice of an engineer on a medical matter, we deemed the opinion of a sole expert on this matter as being preferable to hundreds of opinions from those with no expertise in this field, but who pursue careers in other fields.

As a matter of fact, there is a chaos of terminology today, which is particularly serious when it comes to terms related to

Islam. This stems from various reasons, one of the leading ones being that Muslims interpret Islam in accordance with their own feelings due to the overwhelming helplessness that they have fallen into. The other reason is that some foreigners have attached new meanings to the Qur'an, and the hadith (the Prophet's Traditions, reports of his deeds and sayings), and the most essential Islamic terms and concepts—which have been crystallized and matured through the nurture of these two divine sources—in reference to the culture in which they have grown up, and have disseminated these throughout the world via various means.

Thus, in this work, subjects, such as terrorism, suicide attacks, jihad and others are analyzed in consultation with first-hand sources in the articles written by scientists, every one of who has expertise in different fields of Islamic sciences.

Some passages from a recent interview with M. Fethullah Gülen, a leading and respected Muslim scholar from Turkey, are included at the beginning of the book. His views on terror are particularly worth referring to as he says that "there is no such thing as a Muslim terrorist; a terrorist cannot be a Muslim; a Muslim cannot be a terrorist," and declares that from the point of view of Islamic criteria nobody can justify or permit suicide attacks. This book includes extensive analyses on the following subject matters, in order: i) Islam, always, in all circumstances, approbates peace, ii) the Qur'an regards human life as being exalted and inviolate, iii) Islam considers murder as one of the gravest sins and as a capital crime, iv) in Islam, even in warfare, there are rules to be observed; non-combatant innocent people cannot be killed, v) in the history of wars, Prophet Muhammad, peace and blessings be upon him, was the first person to set forth rules for warfare, vi) Islam regards suicide attacks as heinous murders, and vii) suicide attacks can be perpetrated through use of chemical drugs.

We hope that this book and the articles contained in it will go some way to furthering understanding of Islam's perspective on terror. The only way to put a stop to terrorism and such vio-

lent attacks is to recognize what their true source is. As long as
this issue remains muddied and clouded, for whatever reason,
terrorism cannot be prevented.

Interview with M. Fethullah Gülen

Nuriye Akman

"IN TRUE ISLAM, TERROR DOES NOT EXIST."

Muslims Should Say, "In True Islam, Terror Does Not Exist."

Today, at best we can say that Islam is not known at all. Muslims should say, "In true Islam, terror does not exist." In Islam, killing a human is an act that is equal in gravity to unbelief. No person can kill a human being. No one can touch an innocent person, even in time of war. No one can give a *fatwa* (a legal pronouncement in Islam) in this matter. No one can be a suicide bomber. No one can rush into crowds with bombs tied to his or her body. Regardless of the religion of these crowds, this is not religiously permissible. Even in the event of war—during which it is difficult to maintain balances—this is not permitted in Islam. Islam states; "Do not touch children or people who worship in churches." This has not only been said once, but has been repeated over and over throughout history. What Our Master, Prophet Muhammad, said, what Abu Bakr said, and what 'Umar said is the same as what, at later dates, Salahaddin Ayyubi, Alparslan, and Kılıçarslan also said. Later on, Sultan Mehmet II, the Conqueror, also said the same. Thus, the city of Constantinople, in which a disorderly hullabaloo reigned, became Istanbul. In this city the Greeks did not harm the Armenians, nor did the Armenians harm the Greeks. Nor did the Muslims harm any other people. A short time after the conquest

---

This text has been excerpted from the interview Gülen gave to Nuriye Akman, published in *Zaman* between March 22–April 1, 2004.

of Constantinople, the people of the city hung a huge portrait of the Conqueror on the wall in the place of that of the Patriarchate. It is amazing that such behavior was displayed at that time. Then, history relates that the Sultan summoned the Patriarch and gave him the key to the city. Even today, the Patriarchate remembers him with respect. But today, Islam, as with every other subject, is not understood properly. Islam has always respected different ideas and this must be understood for it to be appreciated properly.

I regret to say that in the countries Muslims live, some religious leaders and immature Muslims have no other weapon to hand than their fundamentalist interpretation of Islam; they use this to engage people in struggles that serve their own purposes. In fact, Islam is a true faith, and it should be lived truly. On the way to attaining faith one can never use untrue methods. In Islam, just as a goal must be legitimate, so must all the means employed to reach that goal. From this perspective, one cannot achieve Heaven by murdering another person. A Muslim cannot say, "I will kill a person and then go to Heaven." God's approval cannot be won by killing people. One of the most important goals for a Muslim is to win the approval of God, another being making the name of Almighty God known to the universe.

The rules of Islam are clear. Individuals cannot declare war. A group or an organization cannot declare war. War is declared by the state. War cannot be declared without a president or an army first saying that there is a war. Otherwise, it is an act of terror. In such a case war is entered into by gathering around oneself, forgive my language, a few bandits. Another person would gather some others around himself. If people were allowed to declare war individually then chaos would reign; because of such small differences a front could be formed even between sound-thinking people. Some people could say, "I declare war against such and such a person." A person who is tolerant to Christianity could be accused as follows: "This man, so and so, helps Christianity and weakens Islam. A war against him should be declared and he must be killed." The result would be that a war is declared. Fortunately, declaring war is not this easy. If the state does not declare a war, no one can wage war. Whoever does this, even if they are scholars whom I admire, does not create a real war; this is against the spirit of Islam. The rules of peace and war in Islam are clearly set out.

An Islamic World, Indeed, Does Not Exist

In my opinion, an Islamic world does not really exist. There are places where Muslims live. They are more Muslims in some places and fewer in others. Islam has become a way of living, a culture; it is not being followed as a faith. There are Muslims who have restructured Islam in accordance with their thoughts. I do not refer to radical, extremist Muslims, but to ordinary Muslims who live Islam as it suits them. The prerequisite for Islam is that one should "really" believe, and live accordingly; Muslims must assume the responsibilities inherent in Islam. It cannot be said that any such societies with this concept and philosophy exist within Islamic geography. If we say that they exist, then we are slandering Islam. If we say that Islam does not exist, then we are slandering humans. I do not think Muslims will be able contribute much to the balance of the world in the near future. I do not see our administrators having this vision. The Islamic world is pretty ignorant, despite a measured enlightenment that is coming into being nowadays. We can observe this phenomenon during the hajj. We can see this displayed during conferences and panels. You can see this in their parliaments through television. There is a serious inequality in the subject matter. They—these Muslims—cannot solve the problems of the world. Perhaps it could be achieved in the future.

Today, there is an Islam of the individual. There are some Muslims in different places of the world. One by one, all have been separated from one another. I personally do not see anyone who is a perfect Muslim. If Muslims are not able to come into contact with one another and constitute a union, to work together to solve common problems, to interpret the universe, to understand it well, to consider the universe carefully according to the Qur'an, to interpret the future well, to generate projects for the future, to determine their place in the future, then I do not think we can talk about an Islamic world. Since there is no Islamic world, every one acts individually. It could even be said that there are some Muslims with their own personal truths. It cannot be claimed that there is an Islamic understanding which has been agreed upon, approved by qualified scholars, reliably based upon the Qur'an, and repeatedly tested. It could be said that a Muslim culture is dominant, rather than Islamic culture.

It has been so since the fifth century AH (eleventh century AD). This started with the Abbasid Era and with the appearance of the Seljuks. It increased after the conquest of Istanbul. In the periods that followed, doors to new interpretations were closed. Horizons of thought became narrowed. The breadth that was in the soul of Islam became narrowed. More unscrupulous people begun to be seen in the Islamic world; people who were touchy, who could not accept others, who could not open themselves to everyone. This narrowness was experienced in the dervish lodges, as well. It is sad that it was even experienced in the *madrasas* (schools of theology). And of course, all of these tenets and interpretations require revision and renovation by cultivated people in their fields.

Al-Qaeda Network

One of the people whom I hate most in the world is [Osama] Bin Laden, because he has sullied the bright face of Islam. He has created a contaminated image. Even if we were to try our best to fix the terrible damage that has been done, it would take years to repair.

We speak about this perversion everywhere on many different platforms. We write books about it. We say, "this is not Islam." Bin Laden replaced Islamic logic with his own feelings and desires. He is a monster, as are the people around him. If there are other people similar to them anywhere, then they too, are nothing more than monsters.

We condemn this attitude of Laden. However, the only way to prevent this kind of deeds is that Muslims living in the countries seeming to be Islamic—and I stated earlier that I do not perceive an Islamic world, there are only countries in which Muslims live—will solve their own problems.

Should they think in a totally different way when electing their leaders? Or should they carry out fundamental reforms? For the growth of a well-developed younger generation, Muslims must work to solve their problems. Not only their problems in the issue of terror, an instrument that is certainly not approved of by God, but also those concerning drugs and the use of cigarettes, two more prohibitions made by God. Dissension, civil turmoil, never-ending poverty, the disgrace of being governed by others, and being insulted after having put up with government by foreign powers are all problems that could be added to the list.

As Mehmet Akif Ersoy said: slavery, a multitude of troubles, addiction, the acceptance of things out of habit, and derision are all commonplace. All of these are anathemas to God, and all of these have been placed primarily on our nation. Overcoming these, in my opinion, depends on being a just human being and a human being who is devoted to God.

Our Responsibility

It is our fault; it is the fault of the nation. It is the fault of education. A real Muslim, one who understands Islam in every aspect, cannot be a terrorist. It is hard for a person to remain a Muslim if he becomes involved in terrorism. Religion does not approve of the killing of people in order to attain a goal.

But of course, what efforts did we make to raise these people as perfect humans? With what kind of elements did we bind them? What kind of responsibility did we take in their upbringing so that now we should expect them not to engage in terror?

People can be protected against becoming involved in terrorism by means of some virtues originating in the Islamic faith, such as, fear of God, fear of the Day of Judgment, and fear of opposing the principles of religion. However, we have not established the required sensitivity on this issue. There have been some minor attempts to deal with this neglected subject to date. But, unfortunately there have been some obstacles put in the way, by our countrymen.

Some say the kind of activities that we need should not be allowed. That is, courses teaching culture and morality should be totally forbidden in educational institutions. At the same time we contend that every requirement of life should be met in schools. Health education should be provided, taught by doctors. Classes related to general life and life in the home should be comprehensively taught in schools.

People should be instructed in how to get along with their future spouses, and how to raise their children. But the issues do not stop here. Both Turkey and other countries that have a large Muslim population suffer from drug abuse, gambling, and corruption. There is almost no one left in Turkey whose name has not been involved in some type of scandal. There are some goals that were supposed to be reached that have been reached. Yet, there are many objectives that still cannot be reached. You cannot question anyone concerning this. You cannot call the people in charge to account. They are protected, sheltered, and thus they have been left alone.

These people are people who grew up among us. All of them are our children. Why have some of them become bad guys? Why were some raised as bullies? Why have some of them rebelled against human values? Why do they come to their own country and blow themselves up as suicide-bombers?

All these people were raised among us. Therefore, there must have been something wrong with their education. That is, the system must have some deficiencies, some weak points that need to be examined. These weak points need to be removed. In short, the raising of human beings was not given priority. In the meantime, some generations have been lost, destroyed, and wasted.

Dissatisfied youth has lost its spirituality. Some people take advantage of such people, giving them a couple of dollars, or turning them into robots. They have drugged them. This has become a topic on the agenda these days which can be read about in magazines. These young people were abused to an extent that they could be manipulated. They have been used as murderers on the pretext of some crazy ideals or goals and they have been made to kill people. Some evil-minded people have wanted to achieve certain goals by abusing these young people.

These people have been turned into robots. Once, many people were killed in Turkey. This group killed that person, another group killed another person. Everyone was involved in a bloody fight before the military came and intervened on March 12, 1971 and later on September 12, 1980. People were almost out for one another's blood. Everyone was killing one another.[1]

Some people were trying to reach a goal by killing others. Everybody was a terrorist. The people on that side were terrorists; the people on this side were terrorists. But, everybody was labeling the same action differently. One person would say, "I am doing this in the name of Islam." Another would say, "I am doing it for my land and people." A third would say, "I am fighting against capitalism and exploitation." These all were just words. The Qur'an talks about such "labels." They are things of no value. But people just kept on killing. Everyone was killing in the name of an ideal.

In the name of these bloody "ideals" many were killed. This was nothing less than terror. Everybody, not only Muslims, was making the same mistake. Since everyone did it, one after another, these killings came to be a goal that was "realizable." Killing became a habit. Everyone began to get used to killing, even

---

[1] Turkey has suffered three military coups in the second half of the twentieth century. The given dates are the second and third, which took place due to unrest in society.

though killing another person is a very evil action. Once, one of my dearest friends killed a snake. He was a theology graduate and he is now a preacher. As a reaction to this action, I did not talk to him for a month. I said: "That snake had a right to live in nature. What right did you have to kill it?"

But today the situation is such that if 10 or 20 people are killed, or if the numbers are not as high as was feared, then we say, "Oh, that's not so bad, not too many have died." This incredible violence has become acceptable by people at a horrible level. "It's good that the number of the death is only 20-30," we say. In short, society as a whole has come to accept this as part of our daily lives.

This situation could have been prevented by education. The laws and regulations of the government could have prevented this. Some marginal groups who are being shielded, and therefore who cannot be stopped, are exaggerating trivial matters, and making important matters insignificant. There is a remedy for this. The remedy is to teach the truth directly. It should be made clear that Muslims cannot be terrorists. Why should this be made clear? Because people must understand that if they do something evil, even if it is as tiny as an atom, they will pay for that both here and in the Hereafter (Zalzala 99:7-8).

Yes, killing a human is a very significant thing. The Qur'an says that killing one person is the same as killing all people. Ibn Abbas said that a murderer will stay in Hell for eternity. This is the same punishment that is assigned to unbelievers. This means that a murderer is subjected to the same punishment as an unbeliever. In short, in Islam, in terms of the punishment to be dealt on the Day of Judgment, a murderer will be considered to be as low as someone who has rejected God and the Prophet (an atheist in other words). If this is a fundamental principle of religion, then it should be taught in education.

ISLAM AS THE RELIGION OF PEACE AND TOLERANCE

İbrahim Canan

With the advent of the means of mass communication and transportation, the world has become a large village. In such a village, unfortunately, it has become easier to influence people, bringing to the fore the power and importance of the media. Once again, unfortunately, in many parts of the world, including Turkey, there have been attempts by the media recently to portray Islam as a religion of terror. In response to this lack of awareness about what Islam is—i.e., this ignorance (and unwillingness to learn as well) on behalf of the media and other influential organizations, which to some extent arises from nothing less than the evil intentions of those who disseminate it and in part due to the fact that Muslims have not been able to represent and introduce Islam in the way that it should have been, it is the duty of the Muslims, once again, to communicate the truth.

The Main Meaning and Basic Characteristics of Islam

The word Islam is derived from the word *silm*, which means reconciliation, peace, submission, and deliverance. Before Islam, all previous revelations had been sent to particular nations. Each of these religions either had the characteristic of being a national religion or was later transformed into a national religion. For the first time in human history Islam came as the religion for all humanity and the Prophet Muhammad, peace and blessings be upon him, was the first to be honored with a duty toward all humanity with Almighty God addressing him as:

> And We have sent you to all the men as nothing but a bearer of good news and as a warner, but most men do not know. (Saba 34:28)

Indeed, the Prophet is a prophet of compassion sent not just for humankind, but for all realms of existence.

> And We have sent you but as a mercy to the worlds. (Anbiya 21:107)

Islam is the religion of unity. That is to say, in the field of faith, this is a religion based on believing only in God, the Lord and Sovereign. Unity, in terms of world vision, the view of life and the social system all call for the unity of humanity, brother and sisterhood, equality in basic rights and the abolition of all discrimination on basis of language, color, race, or family or lineage.

Islam, which heralded the end of national religions in the history of humanity, invites people to live together in freedom within the framework of common laws. Islam has abolished all that belongs to the Age of Ignorance[1] and all that carries the characteristics of that period of ignorance; for example, all egotism, brutality, oppression and injustice; in fact, to a great extent Islam has eradicated these. According to Islam, the dictum "dog eat dog" has been replaced by "love your neighbor"; life is not "a struggle," but a process of "cooperation"; the principle of "let others work while I rest" has been replaced by "support"; "oppression" has left its place to "justice"; "inhumanity" has left its place to "mercy and compassion"; the principle that people have been created free and equal and that people have rights to the

---

[1] The period before the advent of Islam.

degree of their input to society has been instated; the unjust principles of "might has the right" and that "might is right" have been uprooted and the norm of "power is in righteousness, the righteous are powerful" has been put in place; societies have put trust into the rights and justice that belong to the Creator and not to selfish or random laws of a victorious minority or seasoned oppressors.

Islam has declared that all people have honor, with no sociopolitical, material-spiritual, racial-cultural discrimination whatsoever, and has awarded them with a status above all other living things. The Qur'an declares:

> And surely We have honored the children of Adam. (Isra 17:70)

Indeed, according to Islam, even if someone is an unbeliever, his or her possessions, life, or honor cannot be violated. Mental and bodily health and the freedom to form a family are the inalienable rights of every individual. In the same way, no other basic rights and freedoms can be infringed upon. Even in a state of war, women, children, and the elderly who are not fighting are spared. According to the justice brought by the Holy Qur'an, the murder of a single innocent person is a murder that is as heinous as the murder of all humanity. According to Islam, individual rights can in no way be violated, even if to do so were to be for the good of the community. The rights of one single individual are as sacred as the rights of all other people.[2]

Instances of Tolerance from the Past

It is due to the superiority and wisdom that Islam gives people that Muslims have always introduced justice, freedom and humanity wherever they went. Throughout Muslim history, the caliphs, following the example of God's Messenger, gave orders

---

[2] *... whoever kills a soul, unless it be for manslaughter or for mischief in the land, is like one who killed the whole of mankind; and whoever saves a life, is like one who saves the lives of all mankind . . .* (Ma'ida 5:32)

to the commanders they sent to the battlefields that followed the directives given by Abu Bakr to Usama, whom he had sent to Syria (these orders were noted in historical records):

> Usama! Do not betray, inflict injustice, plunder, or defile the bodies; do not kill children, the elderly, or women, do not cut down the date orchards or burn them. Do not cut down trees that bear fruit. Do not kill sheep, cattle, or camels unless it is for food. You may come across people who have retreated into monasteries on your way; do not touch them or interfere with their worship...[3]

It is also fitting that we should remind ourselves of a couple of lines from the text of the treaty that the Prophet signed with the Christians of Najran, providing a perfect example for those Muslims who would follow, until the Judgment Day:

> The protectorate of God and the guardianship of Muhammad are lawful rights unto the people of Najran, those who are ready among them and those who are not, their families (and their affiliates), concerning their possessions, lives, religious lives and practices, and all the things that belong to them. No bishop will be sent outside his region of service, no priest will be sent out of his parish, no monk will be taken out of the monastery where he lives and sent elsewhere . . . they will not be allowed to oppress others, nor will they themselves be oppressed. None among them will be held responsible for any crime and injustice committed by another. (Hamidullah 2003, 1/622)

Once a Christian insulted and cursed the Prophet when he was standing by Gharafa ibn Harith, one of the Prophet's friends and followers. Gharafa, finding this hard to bear, attacked the Christian and during the fight broke his nose. The Christian

---

[3] Ibn Athir, 2/335.

complained to 'Amr ibn al-'As concerning Gharafa. 'Amr ibn al-'As chided Jarafa, saying:

"They were promised safe keeping, why did you do such a thing?"

Gharafa explained: "I didn't think this promise meant that they could curse the Messenger of God. As far as I know they were promised safe-keeping for the following:

1) That we would not interfere with their churches, that they would be able to worship there as they liked,

2) That we would not put them under any obligation that they could not fulfill,

3) That we would fight on their side if an enemy attacked them,

4) That they could resolve their own disputes as they wished,

5) That we would pass judgments according to the orders of God and His Prophet's orders only for those who wanted to be bound by our laws, and we would not force our judgments on those who did not want to be bound by our laws."

Then 'Amr ibn al-'As said to him: "You are right" (Ibn 'Abdulbarr 3/193-194).

In the period of Caliph 'Umar, in AH 14 (635), the city of Humus was conquered. But the following year, when the news reached them that Heracles had prepared an army of 200,000 in order to attack the city, the Muslims decided to evacuate the city. When they were leaving the city they repaid the capitation tax that they have taken from the inhabitants of Humus, and said them the following: "When we took this tax from you, we guaranteed your safety. But now, we will not be able to defend you. You will have to take care of yourselves." The people of Humus, the Christians and the Jews, who knew what it meant to be under Byzantine rule, were not pleased by this situation; on the contrary, they were saddened and the Christian folk said, "Your rule and justice is more favorable to us than the oppression and unlawfulness that we lived under before your arrival. We will join forces with your governor and defend our city against the army of Heracles." The Jews said, "By the Torah! The governor of Heracles will not enter the city of Humus unless he defeats and steps over us."

And so, the local population closed the doors and defended the city. When the armies of Heracles were defeated and had retreated, the local population welcomed the Muslim inhabitants back into the city with open arms. Belazuri, who relates the events, continues thus: "The other Christian and Jewish cities that preferred Muslim rule acted in the same manner and said 'If the Romans and their subjects are victorious over the Muslims, we will continue in the old way. But if only a single Muslim should remain, we will keep to our agreements'" (Belazuri 1987, 187).

Just as the Muslims allowed the members of other religions under their rule to practice their own faith, in the same way they did not object to building mosques, churches, and synagogues side by side, or even Muslims and Christian worshiping in different parts of the same temple. This understanding, which the Prophet started by allotting the Mosque (Masjid al-Nabawi) for the worship of an envoy of Christians from Najran on a Sunday, continued under the first caliphs. Similar practices are reported to have taken place in Cordoba, under the Andalusian Umayyad rule (Özdemir 1994, 1/68). This respect and tolerance toward different beliefs, which is manifested by the co-existence of mosques, churches, and synagogues side by side in some districts of Istanbul, stems from the essence of Islam, from the understanding that Prophet Muhammad has prescribed, peace and blessings be upon him. If this should have been lost with time in some Islamic lands or in some Muslim individuals, then this has nothing to do with Islam; in those cases, one should look for sociological or psychological, regional, or individual causes.

The case of the local population preferring Islamic rule to the rule of their co-religionists is not a one-off incident. There are many such examples. The quotation that the deceased Osman Turan cites from a Christian historian in Urfa is striking: "Melik-şah, who was the most just, wisest, and strongest of all men, was like a father to all people and Christians. All Byzantine natives including Armenians came under his rule of their own volition." (Turan 1969, 2/138)

A Christian writer, who complained of the Islamization of many Christians due to the tolerant and liberal Muslim-Turkish rule which, in turn, made the Byzantines, who had had enough of the plunder, sacking and the oppression committed by the Latins when they came to Istanbul in 1204 on their way to fight the Muslims, "prefer the Turkish turban to the Latin miter in Istanbul," (Turan 1969, 2/153) revealed the nature of Islam and indicated a principle that the Muslims followed when he expressed his discontent:

> Three thousand crusaders, running away from the tyranny of Orthodox Byzantines converted to Islam. Oh you "mercy," you are more tyrant than "betrayal"! For the Turks, by being helpful and compassionate toward the Christians, bought the latter's religion. Nor did they ever force them to convert. (Turan 1969, 2/162)

The right to life, freedom of practicing one's religion, language, law, culture, dress, and tolerance that was shown toward non-Muslims sprang naturally from Islam. In a hadith that tells the Muslim administration to treat non-Muslims well the following is declared: "I am the enemy of any who injures non-Muslims. And whomever I am an enemy to, I will reckon with him on Judgment Day."[4] No Muslim who believes in the Hereafter, would of their own volition, run the risk of reckoning with the Prophet in the afterlife. In another hadith, the following is said:

---

[4] An-Nabahi, 3/144; Ajluni, 2/218.

> Whoever slanders a non-Muslim with adultery, their retribution
> will be lashes of fire on Judgment Day.[5]

In addition, it should be pointed out that non-Muslims were free to apply their own laws concerning matters of justice. This stems from the fact that they are recognized as enjoying freedom of religion. But at the same time, if non-Muslims were to apply to an Islamic court, their cases would be fairly judged. 'The Qur'an says:

> And if you judge, judge between them with equity; surely God
> loves those who judge equitably. (Ma'ida 5:42)

In support of what has just been said, it would be appropriate to quote an imperial edict written by the Ottoman Sultan, Mustafa III, addressed to his Grand Vizier:

> According to the complaints that come from Moldavia and
> Walachia, it appears that you have not concerned yourself with
> the problems of the Christian people living there. In these times
> when there is an effort to send new administrators to Mora and
> the Hijaz, what I desire from my Grand Vizier is to select peo-
> ple from among those who are known to be of high integrity. I
> do not want it to be seen that you have not given due impor-
> tance to this selection because the peoples from these parts have
> different religions and languages. Since they are my subjects I
> would have you know that they have the same rights as my sub-
> jects in Istanbul. Take care not to injure any one of them . . .
> (quoted from *Tercüman* (newspaper), February 9, 1983)

Representing and Communicating Islam

Islam considers humanity to be the most honorable of all creatures, equipped with consciousness and will, and thus recognizes

---

[5] Tabarani, *Al-Mu'jamil al-Kabir*, 22/57.

freedom of belief as an indispensable right. Islam takes the elimination of the obstacles that lie between God and human intellect, consciousness, and will as a fundamental principle. Thus, it stresses the fact that when Islam is introduced, one must follow the route of what can be called "representing and communicating"; the route of practicing and communicating Islam in the best possible way.

For instance, in many verses of the Qur'an, it is declared that there is no other duty that is incumbent on the Prophet and all other prophets other than that of the clear communication of the religion.[6] Moreover, the Prophet is addressed and warned that he is not to exert pressure on people:

> Therefore do remind, for you are only a reminder. You are not a
> watcher over them. (Taghabun 88:22)

Before Islam, some people in Madina, especially if their child survives, would vow to make them "follow the ways of the 'people of the Book'[7] if they survived." This is why at the time of the Prophet some of the children of the pagan people of Madina were "people of the Book." When Islam arrived in Madina some of the families tried to force their children to convert to Islam, upon which the following verse was revealed:

> There is no compulsion in religion; truly the right way has be-
> come clearly differentiated from the erroneous one. (Baqara
> 2:256)[8]

Thanks to these Qur'anic principles, Muslims never forced the local population of the places that they conquered to convert

---

[6] Nahl 16:35, 82; Al 'Imran 3:20; Ma'ida 5:92, 99; Ra'd 13:40; Ibrahim 14:5, etc.
[7] Although *ahl al-kitab*, "People of the Book," is commonly considered to be referring to Christians and Jews, Islamic tradition accepts, in general terms, other belief systems like Zoroastrians, Buddhists, or Hindus under the same category, as their major tenets of faith are similar to that of Islam's.
[8] Az-Zuhayli 1991, 3/20.

to Islam. And some English authors have drawn attention to this aspect of Islam, making the following striking confession: "Had Europeans ruled in Asia instead of Arabs and Turks, there would have been nothing left of the Greek Orthodox Church. And, they would have not practiced the same tolerance toward Islam; the same tolerance that these heathens (i.e., Muslims) have practiced against Christianity." (Toynbee 1978, 285)

Muslims never interfered with the local values of the places they have reached; on the contrary, they preserved them with the awareness of ethnographers. For instance, when the Ottomans left Eastern Europe, North Africa and the Middle East, many nations emerged with their own religions, languages, and traditional clothing.

Islam's Consideration of Humanity

A second reason that keeps Muslims from using force when communicating their religion is their "consideration of mankind," present in the Qur'an.

According to this consideration, humanity has a different nature of creation when compared to other life-forms, such as plants, animals, and angels. People have been created with tendencies toward both good and evil, and have been given reason and understanding; people have also been told to direct themselves toward the good, and to make choices favoring the auspicious, beautiful and good. They have been given both reason and free will to help them make this choice. So, they should distinguish the beautiful and the auspicious with their mind, and choose it with their free will. They have the responsibility to make such choices. The fact that they are creatures that are responsible for their actions stems from these very qualities.

For Muslims, worldly life is a test. In this test, which is undergone in order to achieve the afterlife, the essential thing is to use one's free will. Just as people are not responsible for the sins that they may have been forced to commit, the question of whether or not the good deeds that have been carried out under coercion have any value is one that can be debated. Consequently, coercion has never been applied in the communication of Islam and it never will be.

A Legitimate Objective, Legitimate Means, and Clement Words

Islam stresses the necessity of reaching a legitimate objective through legitimate means and ways. Just like the objective, the ways and means that take us there must also be legitimate. Consequently, Islam will never accept coercion, torture, anarchy, or terror as Islamic means. Moreover, it calls for addressing even tyrants, like the Pharaoh, with clement words when communicating Islam.

The Qur'an expresses this call to Moses and Aaron in the following way:

> Go both to Pharaoh, surely he has transgressed. Speak to him
> gently perchance he may mind or fear. (Ta-Ha 20:43-44)

In one of the verses that determines what the relationship with people of the Book should be, the Qur'an states:

> And do not dispute with the followers of the Book except by
> what is best, except those of them who act unjustly, and say: We
> believe in that which has been revealed to us and revealed to
> you, and our God and your God are One, and to Him do we
> submit. (Ankabut 29:46)

> O followers of the Book! come to a common word between us
> and you that we shall not worship anyone but God and (that) we
> shall not speculate partners with Him, and (that) some of us
> shall not take others for lords besides God (Al Imran 3:64)

We also would like to cite here another verse that can be used in determining the method to be pursued when communicating the true religion to all people, including the people of the Book:

> Call to the way of your Lord with wisdom and goodly exhortation, and have disputations with them in the best manner (Nahl 16:125)

Another verse cites the Prophet's tender treatment of the people he addressed as "a mercy from God" and reminds us that if the Prophet should behave harshly, even those closest to him may leave.[9]

The Prophet placed great importance on persuading people to see the beauty of Islam and in representing Islam in his own person. He used the mosque as a window, a gallery to serve that end. For instance he would welcome foreign groups to the mosque. These people would eat, drink and sleep there and see the Muslims line up for prayer and listen to the recitations of the Qur'an late at night.[10] Sometimes the Prophet would fasten criminals to the pillars of the mosque; these criminals would see the same scenes that we have just described and thus would reform, having undergone an effective education; even those who before were pagan would convert to Islam. There are many individuals who have thus been forgiven and blessed by Islam. Sumama ibn Usal was one of these individuals. Sumama had been involved in a great crime. The Prophet managed to have him caught and bound to a pillar in the Mosque. Three days later Sumama became a Muslim and then went on to be of great service to Islam.[11]

---

[9] *Thus it is due to mercy from God that you deal with them gently, and had you been rough, hard hearted, they would certainly have dispersed from around you . . .* (Al Imran 3:159)

[10] Waqidi 1966, 3/964-65.

[11] Bukhari, *Maghazi*, 70; Muslim, *Jihad*, 59.

"World Peace" and Islam

In order to understand the importance that Islam places on peace we first have to know the aspects and characteristics of the battles in which the Prophet engaged. When we examine these closely we can see that these battles were essentially of a defensive nature.

The first battle waged against the people of Makka was the Battle of Badr. This battle was intended to make the Quraysh tribe, who did not believe in the oneness of God, to realize the great economic importance Madina had for them and thus end their enmity and make them accept peace; it was also intended to help the Muslims reclaim the possessions that had been left in Makka when they left for Madina. These possessions had been put together in a caravan by the Quraysh and sent on its way to be sold in Syria. That is to say, the Muslim's intention in this conflict was the defense of their possessions and the establishment of peace; it was not war for war's sake.

The Battle of Uhud, fought following the Battle of Badr, was a battle started by the people of Makka who came to Madina in order to seek revenge for the former engagement. For the Muslims, this was a purely defensive battle. The Battle of Trench was also a defensive battle that was fought from behind trenches dug around Madina; the aim of this battle was to resist the pagan army, and was fought, not just against the Makkans but against all pagan tribes which were fighting on the side of the Makka.

Almost all of the military campaigns in which the Prophet fought were intended to repel the attacks of the great armies ranged against the Muslims, or in order to prevent the battle preparations of the enemy (the Muslims having received information concerning the same). The Battle of Khaybar, the Battle of Bani Mustaliq, the Tabuk Campaign and many other serious battles and also the battles of Badr, Uhud, and Trench were all battles of one of the two types mentioned here.

The Conquest of Makka, which was one of the most important battles, was an unprecedented effort at attaining both peace and conquest. The city of Makka was conquered on the wisdom of the Prophet and in a peaceful manner: before, during, and subsequent to this conquest 1) the city was not plundered, 2) its people were not killed or exiled, 3) no revenge was taken, 4) no blood feud was pursued.

When the fighting was over, there was a general amnesty, with the exception of a few enemies whose lives had been devoted to active enmity toward Islam and Muslims, and who insisted on continuing on this path; they had tried to resist the conquest with their swords, they had acted outside the boundaries of the conventions of war at that time and had violated commonly recognized laws—that is to say there were a couple of people who, by today's standards, could be categorized as "war criminals." This treatment of the people of Makka was a portrait of honor for humanity, a medal that humanity can proudly bear forever.

Muhammad Hamidullah states that the number of pagans killed during the ten years the Prophet was in Madina was around 250. In that period, the whole of the Arabian peninsula, an area of 1.5 million square miles had submitted to Islam (this would mean a rate of 274 square miles a day!) (Canan 1998, 2/298-301).

The Peace of Hudaybiya and the Concept of Peace in the Qur'an

In order to understand the concept of conquest in the Qur'an, it is sufficient to point out that the Qur'an uses the term conquest when referring to the Peace Treaty of Hudaybiya AH 6 (627). The Prophet set out, accompanied by 1,500 people, to visit the Ka'ba and for the ritual of pilgrimage. But Makkan military units met them in a place near Makka called Hudaybiya, and told them that they were not going to allow the Muslims to visit the Ka'ba. The disputes and negotiations resolved in peace because the Prophet was always on the side of peace.

He believed that there was a need for an environment of dialogue and peace in order for Islam to be understood. According to him, if Islam, which is the genuine faith designed to be one with the nature and common sense of humanity, could be understood in its true nature, surely no one with any common sense would be able to reject it, oppose it, or be its enemy. For that reason, a treaty had to be signed, a platform had to be prepared; that is to say, an atmosphere of ease had to be provided whereby people could set up friendly and commercial relations with Muslims, and thus, experience the life style of the Muslims and get to know Islam at closer quarters. The Makkans, on the other hand, were making a myriad of problems to prevent the institution of a peace; they were trying to put expressions into the treaty that were impossible to accept. But the Prophet accepted some clauses, even though they were rather disturbing for the Muslims, in order to establish peace. For instance, the Muslims were not to enter Makka that year, and could only visit the Ka'ba according to some specific conditions the following year; those who had converted to Islam and sought refuge in Madina were to be returned to the Makkans, and those who wanted to leave the community of Madina and return to Makka were to be released—these were only two of many difficult conditions. The Prophet accepted the treaty all the same, as he was never for war. He was on the side of peace and never doubted the truth of Islam for a second. It is when referring to this treaty that the Qur'an uses the term *a manifest conquest* (Fath 48:1).

Conclusion and a Reminder

It is regretful that some anti-Islamic circles that believe that an atmosphere of peace works for the benefit of Islam do not want the Muslims to live in peace within the non-Muslim world; they strive to make Muslims live in perpetual conflict within the non-Muslim world and maintain an atmosphere of conflict and war. Moreover, these are the circles that perpetually accentuate the names of Muslim leaders who exhibit images that are diametrically opposed to Islam—due to these leaders' misconceptions of Islam—or the administrators of Muslim countries whose relationships with Islam have always been questionable. Consequently, the global population, as a unified body, has to be extremely careful when considering this issue; these are names that have been deliberately portrayed as typical Muslims and this is a critical part of the manipulation and conscious misrepresentation of Islam.

References

Belazuri. *Futuh al-Buldan*, Beirut: 1987

Canan, Ibrahim. *Peygamberimizin Tebliğ Metodları* [The Prophet's Methods in Communicating Islam], Istanbul: 1988.

An-Nabhani, Yusuf. *Al-Futh al-Kabir.*

Hamidullah, Muhammad. *İslam Peygamberi*, Ankara: Yeni Şafak, 2003, Vol. 1, p. 622. Translated by Salih Tuğ. Originally published as *Muhammad Rasulullah*, Paris: Centre Culturel Islamique.

Ibn Abdulbarr, *al-Istiab.*

Ibn Athir, *Al-Kamil Fittarikh.*

Özdemir, Mehmet. *Endülüs Müslümanları* [The Muslims of Andalusia], Ankara: 1994.

Toynbee, Arnold. *Tarihçi Açısından Din*, Istanbul: Kayıhan, 1978. Originally published as *An Historian's Approach to Religion*, London: Oxford, 1956.

Turhan, Osman. *Türk Cihan Hakimiyet Tarihi* [The History of Turkish World Dominance], Istanbul: 1969.

Waqidi, *Maghazi*, Oxford: 1966

ACTS OF TERROR AND SUICIDE ATTACKS
In the Light of the Qur'an and the Sunna

Hamza Aktan

I t is a sad truth that Muslim countries are going through a period when acts of terror threaten their security both at home and abroad. Many negative conditions, such as economic backwardness, social and political dissolution, and cultural degeneration have prepared the ground for the formation of terrorist organizations in the Islamic world, and especially in the countries of the Middle East. It is recognized that some terrorist organizations are supported by various departments of the official administration in the countries where they operate; this is done so that such groups can be used against other terrorist organizations that are active in the same country. It is also another well-recognized fact that, over time, these organizations, made stronger with state support, have grown out of control. Some terrorist organizations, on the other hand, are supported for the political and economic interests of foreign powers, which direct them to particular goals. In this regard, the existence and formation of such organizations are derivatives of various "conspiracy theories"; yet, there is still much that is unclear concerning this issue.

The backwardness of the Islamic world in science and technology, which has been the status quo for the last few centuries, and the consequent backwardness in the economy have resulted in many negative outcomes and weaknesses; most significantly, that of cultural crisis. In this world, where even countries have been divided into blocks, the failure of Islamic countries to form a united front has led them to become mere geographical entities that have left themselves wide open to foreign intervention and exploitation. As a result of the cultural crisis that is being experienced in this part of the world, a proportion of the population regards their intelligentsia and administrators as being alienated and has grown resentful of them. They are harboring growing feelings of rebellion against countries which they consider to be imperialist and against individuals and groups who seem to have interests or relations with these countries. Thus, the fact that terror should breed in such a scenario cannot come as a surprise. In other words, even if the people who lived in this part of the world were not Muslims, under the same circumstances the same reactions would have arisen; in this case, as well, terrorist organizations would have developed. It is a fact that in countries which have not been able to complete the process of development we can see ideological balkanization, i.e., internal conflicts and reactions against imperialist countries, and this reflects the situation that occurs in Muslim countries. Some people and circles interrelate Islamic teachings and the formation of terrorist groups in Islamic countries, calling acts of terror "Islamic terrorism." Others define acts of terror by basing them on the Muslim identity of the terrorist and call them "Islamist terror."

It would be best to leave other aspects of terror to the specialists and to simply discuss the eventuality of terror as related to Islam and Muslims. It is clear that the use of some Islamic values by terrorist organizations and individuals who are parties to acts of terror—principally jihad—as slogans, has resulted in people speculating a relationship between terror and Islam. It is natural that terrorists should want to use every possible means, including religious values, to legitimize their actions in their own eyes and to win public sympathy. Terrorist organizations must certainly use religious values in order to persuade their militant members to commit acts of terror. They see no impropriety in exploiting any value they can. But let us not dwell on this. Our question in this dissertation is whether it is scientifically possible to relate acts of terror, as has been alleged, to the Qur'an and the Sunna (the Prophet's example as recorded in the Traditions), the two essential sources of Islam. In addition, we will investigate analytically whether it is just to dub a terrorist an "Islamist"; to be a terrorist means that one is about as far as one can be from comprehending the basic principles of Islam.

The Concept of Jihad

Since some terrorist groups call their acts jihad, we first have to examine and clarify this concept. Jihad is the name of all effort, exertion, and endurance that each Muslim demonstrates in order to be bestowed with the pleasure of God. In that respect, jihad is a form of worship that will continue without cessation until the end of time. Including the efforts that the individual exerts in subduing the carnal desires, the effort to publicize the beliefs of Islam—which can be done by the learned through their profession, the healthy with their services, and the wealthy financially—and effort and perseverance to protect the honor and integrity of Muslims all are canvassed under the word jihad. Jihad can at times also manifest itself as armed struggle if Muslims are attacked, or when they have clear intelligence that they will be attacked, and are thus obliged to engage the enemy in order to abolish the threat and to protect their integrity and honor.

The number of battles and military engagements that the Prophet himself commanded or sent one of his Companions to command numbers more than sixty. In none of these battles was God's Messenger on the attack. The Prophet never attacked a tribe solely on the basis that they had denied the oneness of God. All the military engagements that he entered were directed at either ending an attack that had already been started, or at stopping such attacks while they were still at the stage of preparation. The verses that encourage Muslims toward jihad were revealed concerning an unpreventable war that had already started. So, according to the Qur'an and the Sunna the essential element of international relations is peace. War is an exceptional situation.

Wars that are waged to protect the existence and honor of Muslims are only small links in the chain that makes up the process of jihad; a chain that stretches to eternity. In this regard, jihad that manifests itself as war in circumstances of self-defense is a legitimate tool. It is permissible for Muslims to react to an invasion of their country, or to exploitation and oppression, and that they should fight against these; moreover, it is their most natural right and ultimate responsibility. But there is a very important matter that must be taken into account here: just as in any other legal system, the basic principle in Islamic law is that, just as the goal must be legitimate, so too must the means through which one reaches that goal. It is for this reason that the Qur'an does not merely encourage Muslims to resist and fight, but also tells them how war should be waged.

Can one call jihad the killing of civilians, women, children, and the elderly, shooting into school buses with machine guns, burning houses, shops, and cars, kidnapping, and even killing people who have no relation to a specific incident? And what if the people killed and whose property has been damaged are Muslims? If the organizations that carry out these acts did not receive orders from one central authority, if they answer to no authority for what they have done and if they act only according to their personal wishes, how then can their acts be considered as jihad? Is it enough that people who detonate explosives hidden on their persons or in their cars to call themselves *mujahids* (the doers of jihad)? Is merely calling the acts they commit jihad enough for these people to be *mujahids* and for their acts to be jihad? Readers can decide for themselves whether these acts can be called jihad and whether those who commit them can be called *mujahids* based upon the examples below. Let us try to clarify the issue by giving examples from some acts of the Prophet, acts which form the basis for Islamic Rules of Engagement.

Rules Concerning the Aspect of War in Jihad

The rules concerning the aspect of jihad that is concerned with war in Islam can be summarized under the following headings that are based on the Sunna of the Prophet and taken in the light of the Qur'an:

1. Treating the enemy with mercy

The Prophet never intended to crush the enemy, neither physically nor psychologically, under any circumstances, even in a time of war. We have learned from the Prophet that we have to show mercy to people when they are in a state that invokes our mercy and that calls for our pity, even if these people are our enemies. In AH 8 (629), in the month of Shawwal in the lunar calendar, the Prophet sent Khalid ibn Walid to fight the tribe of the Bani Jazima with a force of 300 men. He told Khalid ibn Walid not to wage war against them unless they were attacked first. When the Bani Jazima saw the forces of Khalid ibn Walid, they took up arms. During battle, a young man from a good family was killed in front of the woman he loved by the Muslim forces. The woman collapsed upon the man and she sobbed twice. Her heart stopped beating due to the deep sorrow she felt and she died, holding the dead man. This incident was later recounted to the Prophet. The Prophet was saddened and he said "Was there no one who had mercy among you?" When he was informed that Khalid had killed some of the prisoners of war he raised his two hands to the sky and pleaded, "Dear God! I swear to you that I am in no way involved in what Khalid has done. I did not order him to do so!" (Ibn Kathir 1976, 3/591)

After the conquest of the Khaybar Castle, Safiyya binti Huyay and her cousin were escorted to the Prophet by Bilal, passing among the dead of the Jews on the way. When Safiyya's cousin saw the corpses of her relatives she started to wail and struck her face with her hands. The Prophet remonstrated with Bilal: "O, Bilal! Has the feeling of mercy so abandoned your heart that you have led these women to where the corpses were?" Bilal said "Prophet of God! I did not know that you would not approve." As is known, the Prophet invited Safiyya binti Huyay to convert to Islam and when she accepted, he márried her; in this way Safiyya attained the honor of becoming a mother of believers.[1]

2. The ban on torture

The Prophet did not allow the enemy to be tortured in any way. Suhayl ibn 'Amr was one of the prominent individuals of Makkan pagans. He was among those who had insulted and oppressed the Prophet before his Emigration to Madina. He was taken as a prisoner of war in the Battle of Badr. At one point he tried to escape, but was caught and taken back. Suhayl was a good speaker. He was capable of influencing people with his words. 'Umar said to the Prophet: "O, Messenger of God! Allow me to take out his two front teeth so that he will not be able to speak against you again." To which the Prophet replied: "No, I will not have him tortured. If I did, God would punish me. Moreover, we should always have the hope that one day he will act in a way that will not seem unsympathetic to you."[2] Indeed, after the death of the Prophet, when there were cases of apostasy in Makka, Suhayl ibn 'Amr called out to the Makkans "O, Makkans! You were the last to accept the religion of God. Do not let yourselves now be among the first to leave it." and thus prevented many people of Makka from leaving Islam.[3]

Nabbash ibn Qays, a Jew from the Bani Qurayza tribe, who had been sentenced to death due to his treachery in the Battle of the Trench was brought before the Prophet. Nabbash's nose had been broken. The Prophet remonstrated with the person who had brought him: "Why did you do this to him? Is it not enough that

---

[1] Ibn Hisham 1971, 3/350-351; Waqidi 1966, 2/673.
[2] Ibn Hisham 1971, 2/304; Tabari 1967, 2/465, 561.
[3] Ibid.

he will be killed?" The man made the following excuse: "He pushed me in order to escape. We had a scuffle."[4]

Eight people came to Madina, saying they wanted to become Muslims. They were ill and were in need of help. Madina's air worsened their health. The Prophet sent them to the pasture where the camels of *zakat*[5] were kept. They stayed there for about three months and recovered their health. Then they cut off the hands and feet of the shepherd who was looking after the camels, stuffed thorns into his eyes and tongue and tortured him to death. They also took away the camels. When the news reached Madina, 20 horsemen were immediately sent after them under the command of Kurz ibn Jabir. The horsemen arrested all the criminals and brought them back to Madina. They were found guilty of robbery, murder, treachery, and apostasy. They were punished on the order of the Prophet,[6] who after this event banned the use of torture, whatever the cause may be.[7]

3. Respecting the enemy's dead

Pagans at the time of the Prophet had the habit of mutilating the bodies of the people they killed in battle, and disemboweling them for revenge. This act was known as *musla*. When the Prophet saw the disemboweled and defiled body of his uncle Hamza during the Battle of Uhud, he was deeply saddened. He said "If God allows me victory, I will do the same to thirty pagans in return for what they have done to Hamza." Upon this the following verse was revealed:

---

[4] Köksal 1981, 1/353.
[5] *Zakat* is one of the five foundations of Islam. Every believer is required to bestow a portion of their property in alms. *Zakat* of camels is due upon at least five camels, and it is one goat or sheep, provided they subsist upon pasture throughout the year.
[6] Bukhari, *Hudhu*, 17-18; Muslim, *Qusama*, 9-11.
[7] Waqidi, 2/570; Köksal 1981, 13/127.

> And if you have to respond to any wrong, respond to the extent
> done to you; but if you endure patiently this is indeed better for
> he who endures. (Nahl 16:126)

The Prophet renounced his oath and paid the appropriate amount for atonement as set down by Islamic law.[8] To Abu Qatada, enraged by the *musla* carried out on Hamza and who was about to perform the same to the bodies of the pagans, the Prophet said: "Sit down! Wish for the reward you will get from God! The dead of the Qurayshi pagans are entrusted to our care . . . Would you rather your name was remembered with what you did and resented along with what they have done?"[9]

While the Makkan army was approaching Madina to confront Muslims at Uhud, they arrived at the village of Abwa, where the grave of the Prophet's mother, Amina, was. Some of them suggested that they should dig up the grave and take her bones with them. "If Muhammad gets hold of our women, we could use these bones to barter with, and give him these bones back if he gives us our women. If no such situation arises, he will pay a high price for the return of these bones." But those with commonsense said, "No, this would not be right. If we do such a thing, the people of Huzaa and the Bani Bakr will dig up the bones of our dead in return." And thus they had enough foresight not to start an evil tradition.[10]

4. Not attacking civilians and innocent targets

The fact that the Prophet warned his friends and followers many times about sparing the lives of those who were not involved in a war has been often cited in the literature of both *tabaqat*[11] and *maghazi*.[12]

---

[8] Ibn Hisham, 3/101; Haythami, 6/120.
[9] Waqidi, 1/290.
[10] Ibid, 1/206.
[11] *Tabaqat*: A general name for books which study contemporaneous scholars, members of the same school of thought or a Sufi group covering a time frame of 10-20 years.

After the conquest of Makka, and the Quraysh's submission to Islam, the Hawazin, especially Bani Hanifa, who regarded themselves as the greatest tribe after Quraysh, called for war against Muslims, and they were supported by the tribe of Thaqif. At the end of the battle which was joined at Hunayn, the Prophet saw the body of a dead woman among the dead of the pagans. "What is this that I see?" he asked. Those who were present answered: "This is a woman, killed by the forces of Khalid ibn Walid." The Prophet said to one of them "Run to Khalid! Tell him that the Messenger of God forbids him to kill children, women, and servants." One of those present said "Dear Messenger of God! But are they not the children of the pagans?" The Prophet answered: "Were not the best of you, too, once the children of pagans? All children are born with their true nature and are innocent."[13]

At a time near the death of the Prophet, when he was gravely ill, news came that the Northern Arabs, along with the Byzantine, were preparing an attack on Madina. The Prophet immediately ordered for the preparations of an army and appointed Usama ibn Zayd as the commander. He gave the following instructions to Usama: "Fight in God's path, fight for God. Fight the aggressors who deny God. Do not be cruel to people. Do not go against your covenant. Do not cut down fruit bearing trees. Do not slaughter livestock. Do not kill the pious who are secluded in monasteries, engaged in worship, children, or women. Do not wish to encounter the enemy. You may not be aware of it, but you may face a test with them."[14]

The Prophet decided to send a force of fifteen people to the Ghatafan tribe, who were in the alliance against Muslims at the Battle of Muta. He appointed Abu Qatada as the commander of

---

Tabaqat has mainly been studied under the domain of hadith. The first book of *Tabaqat* is Ibn Sa'd's *Al-Tabaqat al-Kubra*, which gave accounts of the lives of the Companions and their followers (*tabi'un*).

[12] *Maghazi*: Books on the military campaigns of the Prophet.

[13] Abu Dawud, *Jihad*, 111.

[14] Waqidi, 3/117-118.

the unit. He ordered him "Do not kill women and children!" Likewise, the Prophet decided to send a force of seven hundred upon the people of Dumat al-jandal, who were reported to be preparing for an attack. To 'Abd al-Rahman ibn al-'Awf, whom he had appointed as the commander of the unit, he gave the following order: "Do not spoil the goods that you have seized, do not go against your covenant, and do not amputate the organs of the corpses. Do not kill children. This is the covenant you have made with God and it is the way of His Prophet."[15]

One of the most striking examples of this was the behavior of Hubayb ibn Adiyy. Abu Bara', the leader of the tribe of Amir came to Madina in AH 4 (625). He requested that he be allowed to take some people who could teach Islam to the people of Najid and he said he would stand as guarantor for the life of these people. Upon his word, the Prophet sent 40 people (according to some reports, 70) under the command of Munzir ibn 'Amr.[16] But Amir ibn Tufayl, the nephew of Abu Bara', did not honor the guarantee of his uncle.

Amir ibn Tufayl requested help from some branches of the Bani Sulaym tribe. He besieged the group of teachers in Bi'r al-Mauna and almost all of them were martyred.[17] Hubayb ibn Adiyy and Zayd ibn Dassina were taken to Makka as prisoners and were sold to the pagans of the Quraysh, who were in a crazed state, seeking revenge for their dead. Hubayb ibn Adiyy was shackled with chains on his feet. He was waiting to be killed. He asked for a razor from a freed slave woman named Mawiya in order to shave and clean himself. Mawiya gave a razor to her three year old stepson and said "Go give this to the prisoner." Mawiya recounts what followed thus: "The boy brought the razor to the prisoner. I said to myself 'Dear God, what have I done?' and ran after the boy. When I arrived near them I saw the boy sitting on Hubayb's lap and talking to him, and I cried out. Hu-

---

[15] Ibn Hisham, 4/280-281.
[16] Köksal 1981, 35.
[17] Ibid. 41.

bayb looked at me and said: 'Do you fear that I will kill this child? God forbid that I should ever commit such an act. Taking life for no reason is not our manner of behavior and is unfitting to our name. You are not the ones who want to kill me.'" They took Hubayb ibn Adiyy and Zayd ibn Dassina to Tanim, a distance of 10 kilometers from Makka and killed them there with spears.[18]

All of the above examples given here are nothing more than the application of the basic principle of jihad, a principle that has been immutably established in the Qur'an: fight only those who fight and do not attack civilian or innocent targets that are not engaged in the war:

> And fight in the way of God with those who fight with you, and do not trespass the limits, surely God does not love those who trespass the limits. (Baqara 2:190)

> O you who believe! Be upright for God, bearers of witness with justice, and let not hatred of a people incite you to act unjustly; act justly, which is nearer to piety, and be careful of (your duty to) God; surely God is Aware of what you do. (Ma'ida 5:8)

Treating the enemy without mercy, committing *musla*, torture, killing women and children means going beyond the boundaries, the legitimate limits that have been set; that is why they all have been forbidden by God in the verses quoted above.

5. Not targeting Muslims

Having established that it is forbidden to kill innocent non-Muslims, even during war, it is inconceivable to think that it would be permissible to kill innocent Muslims under any circumstances. Whether Muslims can fire against the enemy who are shielding themselves with Muslim captives is still a topic of de-

---

[18] Bukhari, *Maghazi*, 28; Ibn Hajar 1328; 1/418.

bate among scholars of Islamic law—even if not shooting means defeat and the utmost care is taken not to hit the Muslim captives.

During the lifetime of the Messenger of God there was never a case of Muslims killing Muslims in a state of war. There was only once such an incident, and this was the result of error and misunderstanding. During the incident of Bi'r al-Mauna, recounted above, 'Amr ibn Umayya, one of the teachers taken prisoner, was freed as part of the fulfillment of an oath. On the way back to Madina he killed two people from the tribe of the Bani 'Amr, thinking they were the enemy. In fact, they had recently converted to Islam, and their lives had been guaranteed by the Prophet. The Prophet was greatly saddened by this incident. He paid the blood money of these people who had been killed.[19]

After the conquest of Makka, Harith ibn Dhirar, a member of the Bani Mustaliq tribe, came to Madina and became Muslim. He also played an important role in his whole tribe becoming Muslim. The Prophet appointed Walid ibn Uqba for the collection of taxes from the tribe of Bani Mustaliq. The people of Bani Mustaliq who saw Walid went out to welcome him as the official of the Prophet of God. Walid was frightened to see them come toward him and returned to Madina, saying to the Prophet: "Prophet of God! The Bani Mustaliq have prevented me from collecting the taxes. They wanted to kill me. They gathered together to fight you." The Prophet sent Khalid ibn Walid to investigate the situation. It was understood that things were not as Walid ibn Uqba had understood them to be.[20] Concerning this incident the following verse was revealed:

> You who believe! If an evil-doer comes to you with a report,
> look carefully into it, lest you harm some people unwittingly,
> then be sorry for what you have done. (Hujurat 49:6)

---

[19] Ibn Sa'd, 2/53; Waqidi, 1/351-352.
[20] Ahmad ibn Hanbal 1985, 4/279; Zurkani 1973, 3/47.

All-Just God never condoned the killing of Muslims by Muslims in the battlefield, even in error. In AH 6 (627), the Prophet arrived at Hudaybiya near Makka with his followers, on their way to perform *umra* (minor pilgrimage). The pagans of Makka did not allow them into the city. Upon this, the Prophet put his seal to a treaty that guaranteed a ten-year peace. In the treaty were clauses that were adverse for the Muslims, but the Prophet chose to sign it with his own seal rather than go to war. Thus, imminent war was prevented. One of the hidden truths of the Hudaybiya Peace Treaty is explained in the Qur'an as follows:

> And were it not for the believing men and the believing women, whom, not knowingly, you might have trodden down, and thus something hateful might have afflicted you on their account without knowledge—so that God may cause to enter into His mercy whomsoever He pleases; had they been widely separated one from another, We would surely have punished those who disbelieved from among them with a painful punishment. (Fath 48:25)

That is, by Hudaybiya Treaty, the unwitting killing of Muslims in Makka and an armed struggle, which would have resulted in much bloodshed, were prevented. God did not condone the idea of Muslim soldiers killing any Muslims who may not have been able to leave Makka. But today, Muslims are knowingly killed as a result of acts that some call jihad. How can one possibly think that God would condone such acts?

6. Acting within the hierarchy of order and command

Another very important principle concerning the aspect of war in jihad is to act according to a centralized plan accepted by all Muslims. If individuals or groups should act without taking orders from a central authority, if they should act according to their own discretion, the fact that they are not responsible to anyone for their actions will result in chaos. Even if central authority has been lost, this cannot justify acting in a disparate or irresponsible manner. Chaos cannot possibly be condoned in the name of jihad. In these situations, it is highly probable that any movement will degenerate, become diverted from its original goal, and cause more harm than good.

In the Age of Happiness, no act of jihad, in terms of armed struggle, occurred without the Prophet's order or permission. There have only ever been a few incidents of this kind where conflicts arose due to misunderstanding. These incidents grieved the Prophet, and their perpetrators were warned. He chided 'Abd Allah ibn Jahsh for doing something that he was not ordered to do; Khalid ibn Walid was warned against killing women and children; 'Amr ibn Umayya paid the blood money of the Muslims that he killed.

Even the incident involving Abu Basir is no exception to this rule. Abu Basir was from the Bani Thakif tribe. After becoming a Muslim he was imprisoned by the Makkan pagans. He found the opportunity to escape after the Hudaybiya Treaty and came to Madina, seeking refuge within the Islamic community. According to the Hudaybiya Treaty, the Muslims in Madina were not to provide refuge for Makkans who had become Muslims and fled to Madina. Two people came from Makka to collect Abu Basir.

The Prophet obeyed the clauses of the treaty and handed Abu Basir over to the Makkans. Saddened by the situation Abu Basir was comforted by the Prophet: "Abu Basir! Go now. God will provide a consolation and a way out for you and those like you" (Ibn Hisham 1971, 3/337). Abu Basir killed one of the two people who were taking him to Makka. The other one fled. Abu Basir came back to Madina and said to the Prophet: "O Prophet of God! You have kept your promise. And God rescued me from their hands." The Prophet replied: "You are amazingly brave! If you have some men with you, perhaps, no one will be able to stop you. Go now, wherever you will" (Waqidi 1966, 2/626-

627). Abu Basir took some men with him and garrisoned them in the coastal town of Is, which is located on the caravan route from Makka to Damascus. People who had converted to Islam and who were not able to seek refuge in Madina gathered around Abu Basir. They did not let any Makkan caravans pass. It was the Makkans themselves who at last went to Madina and asked the Prophet to accept Abu Basir and his friends into the Islamic community there. It was then that the Prophet called Abu Basir and his friends to Madina. Abu Basir had to protect himself and he succeeded; he had no intention of acting independently. When the written order from the Prophet calling him to Madina arrived, he was on his death bed. After he was buried, according to the written order of the Prophet, seventy of his friends returned to Madina, while the remaining ones returned home (Ibn Abdulbarr, 4/20; Diyarbakri, 2/25).

7. Humanitarian aid to the enemy

Jihad does not always mean that the enemy must be harmed. Helping the enemy in moments of dire need is within the scope of jihad. Such behavior can also lessen enmity, and break down the resolve of the enemy.

In the years of draught and famine in Makka after the Muslims left for Madina, the Prophet sent gold to Makka so that they could buy wheat, dates, and animal feed; these contributions helped them to make up the cash shortage. Even though the leading pagans of the Quraysh, like Umayya ibn Halaf and Safwan ibn Umayya, did not want to accept this aid, Abu Sufyan voiced his gratitude in the following manner: "May God reward the son of my brother with favors, for he has taken into consideration the dues of kinship" (Köksal 1981, 14/304).

Another example of helping the enemy is the incident of Sumama ibn Usal from the Yamama tribe. After becoming a Muslim, Sumama paid a visit to Makka. The pagans understood from the prayers and verses he was reciting that he was a Muslim; they captured him and tried to kill him. But some of the leading figures of the pagans ordered his release, stating that to do otherwise would cut off the food supply from the Yamama. When Sumama returned to his homeland of Yamama, he cut off the supply of food to Makka. The Makkans found themselves in a very difficult situation. They sent envoys to the Prophet, asking him to order Sumama not to cut off the supply of food to Makka. With a written order, the Prophet ordered Sumama to cease his blockade. And so Sumama let his people start to send food to the Makkans.[21]

8. War as the last resort

Using force in the context of jihad is not always the right thing to do. The fact that armed conflict was not allowed until the Battle of Badr attests to this fact. In the second 'Aqaba Pledge,[22] which took place three months before the Prophet's emigration to Madina, Abbas ibn Ubada said "O, the Prophet of God! I swear by God who sent you with the true faith and the Book, if you should ask me, we shall put all the people in Mina to the sword." Although the Prophet had suffered at the hands of the people of Makka who came to 'Aqaba for the fair, he answered: "This is not what we have been ordered to do; now return to your goods." This should be sufficient to make it clear that the response to oppression, insult, and torture need not always be crude force.

Why did the Prophet remonstrate with Abdullah ibn Jahsh, who had been sent on an intelligence mission to the ramparts of Makka in the seventeenth month of the Prophet's emigration, and who had attacked a caravan belonging to the Quraysh, killing some people and taking others prisoner? Clearly, it is both because this act was committed during, Rajab, one of the sacred

---

[21] I. Hisham 4/228.
[22] 'Aqaba is a location at the entrance of a valley located between two hill ranges leading to Mina, near Makka, where an annual fair took place. The Prophet met people from Madina at 'Aqaba, and they swore allegiance to him and pledged to protect him whatever the cost.

months when fighting was prohibited, and because the conditions for engaging in war with the Quraysh and their affiliates had not yet been fully determined.

The righteousness of the policy held by the Prophet was soon proven when he put his seal under the treaty of Hudaybiya, as explained above (Fath 48:25). Makka was conquered after two years of patience, with no bloodshed, due to this policy which was based primarily on peace. The invaluable Sunna of the Prophet proves that reaching a goal through other means than armed conflict is possible.

The Prophet abandoned the siege of Taif, which promised to be a long one, to prevent the deaths of women and children, who would be at the receiving end of the blind shots of the catapults; he wanted to prevent many deaths on both sides. This was a wise policy and strategy that allowed for the goal to be reached with no battle being engaged; the result was that the people of Taif— people who realized their homeland become an isolated island of unbelievers in the Arabian peninsula—came to Madina before the end of the same year, saying that they had converted to Islam.

In short, the acts of those who kill civilians, women, children and the elderly on crowded streets of our cities, those who burn or bomb vehicles and buildings, those who torture and kill people that they have kidnapped or taken as hostage, the acts of suicide bombers who kill themselves and innocent people with explosives placed on their persons or in automobiles—all of these acts, for which no legal authority is responsible—cannot be seen as being jihad and these people cannot be seen as being *mujahids*. There is no foundation for these acts in either the Qur'an or the Sunna. What is important is the structure and character of a thing; it does not matter what people call it. There is no way that Muslims could have come up with such a bloody and contaminated form of struggle in order to make their voices heard. Rather, this is a method that was principally adopted by non-Muslim anarchist terrorist groups. These acts have not helped Muslims in any way to date. On the contrary, they have destroyed the good image of Islam—an image which is founded on science and knowledge, rights and justice, love and peace. At the same time, these acts have led people to postulate a connection between Islam, Muslims, and terrorism. These actions, known as jihad, have done more harm to Islam than anything else could have done.

As has been analyzed above in detail, terror has no place in the varying aspects of jihad. The conditions under which Muslims should behave and how they should behave, and how and with whom they should engage in combat have all been strictly established by the Qur'an and the Sunna. No Muslim can be a true Muslim and at the same time diverge from or go against the path that God and His Prophet have established.

References

Ahmad ibn Hanbal. *Al-Musnad*, Beirut: 1985.

Bukhari, Abu 'Abdullah Muhammad ibn Ismail. *Al-Jami' al-Sahih*, Istanbul: 1981.

Diyarbakri, Husayn ibn Muhammad ibn al-Hasan. *Tarikh al-Hamis fi Ahwal al-Anfas al-Nafs*, Beirut.

Abu Dawud, Sulayman ibn Ash'as al-Sijistani. *Sunan Abu Dawud*, Beirut: 1971.

Ibn Abdilbarr, *Al-Istiab fi Marifat al-Ashab*.

Ibn Hajar, Ahmad ibn Ali. *al-Isaba fi Tamyiz as-Sahaba*, Beirut: AH 1328 (1910).

Ibn Hisham, Abu Muhammad Abdulmalik. *Al-Sirat al-Nabawiyya*, Beirut: 1971.

Ibn Kathir, Abu'l Fida Ismail. *Al-Seerah al-Nabawiyya*, Beirut: 1976.

Ibn Sad, at-Tanaktu'l Kubra, Beirut, 1985.

Köksal, M. Asım. *İslam Tarihi*, Istanbul: 1981.

Muslim, Ibn Hajjaj al-Kushayri. *Sahih al-Muslim*, Istanbul, 1981.

Tabari, *Tafsir*, Egypt: 1954.

Waqidi, Muhammad ibn 'Umar. *Kitab al-Maghazi*, Oxford University Press, 1966.

Zurkani, Muhammad. *Sharh al-Mawahib*, Beirut: 1973.

RELIGION, TERROR, WAR, AND THE NEED FOR GLOBAL ETHICS

Bekir Karlığa

Terror, which manifested itself as a means of rebellion against the unipolar world that emerged after the collapse of the Soviet Union, has become a global catastrophe with the advent of September 11th. The fact that the only sovereign power which has set out to fight terrorism considers the situation to be a cause for war, has not only made humanity—and more especially the Middle East—come face to face with the threat of war once again, but it has also led to the neglect or rejection of human values. Consequently, the principles of "universal ethics" and "international law," which are the aims of the United Nations, an institution that was set up after the harrowing experiences of two great wars, have been violated and unease of global proportions has arisen. In the face of these developments, religious and ethical values have once again regained great importance.

Religion

Religion may be roughly defined as the sum of the rules and principles that have been sent by God to guide humanity to happiness in this world and in the hereafter.

The history of religion starts with the history of humanity. The first explanations by people concerning what went on around them—near or far—were based on religion. This led to religion playing a very important role in the arenas that humanity have cultivated in the course of history, such as science, culture, art, law, and ethics.

Religion makes it possible for people to discover the lofty and transcendent values that are hidden deep in their nature and thus to experience a special delight.

Ideas that do not somehow converge with religion perforce remain one-dimensional and lack the capacity to explain existence as a whole. On the other hand, a religion which has no wisdom results in the individual being entrapped in constricted molds and to a loss in the value of life, rather than the intended aim, i.e., the opening and surmounting of one's horizons.

Just as people are not able to determine their own identity without a belief, nor are they able to grasp their place, role, and status in this universe. It is a clear fact that humankind is the most valuable and important creation of the universe. The element that enables people to possess such importance and worth is our spiritual structure, not our physical structure. With regard to our physical makeup, we share many characteristics with other creatures. Like other organisms, our bodies are also made up of cells, genes, and tissues. But what makes us special is our ability to think, believe, and acquire knowledge, and the fact that we are aware of these capabilities; that is to say humans are conscious beings. It is due to this quality that we can make abstractions and formulate general concepts, and also that we are able to determine thoughts and actions. These values form beliefs and norms.

The spiritual and physical makeup (the soul and body) of humankind form a complete entity. False beliefs and rigid ideologies are trying to rip apart this entity: they have either tried to make people into abstract beings with only souls, or into physical beings composed of only bodies. This in turn has led to the creation of misconceptions about existence as a whole. The essential goal of divine religions is to bring together this sundered existence within the framework of "knowledge and wisdom." But sometimes even religions become removed from their essence and are turned into dogmas; this is when they fail to perform the principle mission for which they have been created. When this occurs, religions either turn into a rigid ideology or into a collection of hollow rituals.

According to the renowned Islamic scholar, Imam Shatibi (d. 790), the principle aim of religion is the benefit of humanity in this world and in the hereafter. Consequently, included among the main objectives of religion are the preservation of faith, life, wealth, progeny, and mind:

> In all religions, the responsibilities conferred upon mankind are there in order to protect the following three things: the Requisites (*Az-Zaruri*), the Necessary (*Al-Haji*) and those that ameliorate (*At-Tahsini*).
>
> The Requisites (*Az-Zaruri*) connote those things that have to be present if one is to realize benefits, in both the religious and the secular aspects of life. . . This is so true that if they are lost, worldly functions cannot be performed; and these functions deteriorate, anarchy rules, and sometimes this can even lead to the end of life. Likewise, salvation in the hereafter is lost, as well as any gifts that have been bestowed, and disappointment is the final result. (Faith, life, mind, progeny, and wealth are the requisites that need protection from danger—Ed.)
>
> The protection of the requisites can be achieved in the one of the following two ways: The first way is to lay sturdy foundations and to keep the pillars strengthened—this means keeping them well maintained by means of those elements that are already present in life. The other method is to take care of any deficiencies; that is, to keep the requisites well maintained by taking measures that will prevent these elements from disappearing. For instance, faith, the testimony of faith, giving alms, the hajj, fasting, and other similar ways of worship are directed toward the protection of religion as existing phenomena. Eating, drinking, clothing, lodging, and similar habits are directed toward the protection of the mind and the soul as existing phenomena. Public behavior is aimed at the protection of one's be-

longings and progeny; while habits or behavior patterns are intended to protect the health of the mind and the soul through establishing certain treatment patterns. Punishments, which are aimed at encouraging good deeds and preventing bad deeds, provide protection by means of keeping certain negative elements out of the realm of both society and the individual. There are five essential goals of the *Shari'a*. These are the preservation of faith, life, wealth, progeny, and mind. It is stated that in all religions these basic elements are considered to be essential rights that must be protected.

The Necessary (*al-Haji*) are those things that are needed in order to eradicate the difficulties and problems that generally arise as a result of the loss of general physical or metaphysical wishes of people, both in personal and social perspectives. If these needs are not attended to, then all those responsible will face difficulties and run into problems. But the difficulties mentioned here—which occur when these needs (needs may be material or abstract) are not attended to—are not to the same degree as the degeneration caused by the injury committed against common benefit. These things that could be placed in the circle of the Requisites are but only to mention in the realms of worship, habit, behavior, and punishment. (Dry ablution for those who cannot find water, being free from fasting when on a journey, or praying while seated for those who cannot physically unable to stand, can be considered among the Necessary—Ed.)

The elements directed towards Amelioration (*at-Tahsini*), on the other hand, can be formulated as adopting the appropriate and good habits, and staying away from the shameful and the evil ones which people with common sense would abstain from. All of these kinds of behaviors, too, are classified and labeled as "public moral virtues," and the conditions that are valid for the first two issues (the Requisites and Necessary) are also valid for this one. (Shatibi 2/4)

Thus, it is impossible for there to be a concept of religion where one of these three universal principles of religion is neglected. But unfortunately, both in the past and today, religion and values that are considered sacred by religion seem to lie behind negative phenomena, such as aggression, terror, and war. In fact, what injures religions most—and it does indeed—is this bitter reality. In order to remedy this negative situation and to save religions from being used as a reason for enmity, the leaders of world religions must come together and take steps toward inter-religious peace, tolerance, and dialog.

Terror

Terror is a crime against humanity. "Religion" and "terror" are two concepts that can never be brought together, for all religions deny and condemn terror. Terror is not just one crime unto itself; within it are contained five other crimes. A terrorist commits a crime against the Creator, against humanity as a species, against the particular individuals at whom the terror is directed, against themselves, and against the community of which they are a member.

According to Islam, humanity, which has been *honored* (Isra 17:70), has been created by God *in the best form and nature* (Tin 95:4). Since *the One who gives life and death is God* (Al 'Imran 3:156), it is forbidden to kill: *Do not kill the soul which God has made sacred, except for a just cause* (An'am 6:151); no one can take away the life that God has given. Thus, *whoever kills a soul, unless it be for manslaughter or for mischief in the land, is like one who killed the whole of mankind* (Ma'ida, 5:32).

Moreover, according to the verse *And spend in the way of God and cast not yourselves to perdition with your own hands, and do good (to others); surely God loves the doers of good* (Baqara 2:195) no one has the right even to put oneself in danger, nor, according to the following verse does anyone have the right to kill oneself: *Nor kill (or destroy) yourselves: for verily God has been to you Most Merciful* (Nisa 4:29). Consequently, whatever the grounds may be, in Islam "the prohibition of damage to oneself or to others" is a general rule; the killing of innocent people is an unforgivable crime against humanity.

In Islam, rights are divided into three different categories: "the rights of God," "the rights of people," and "composite rights"; the first two play a major role.

The rights of God are generally considered to be belief in God and worshiping Him, along with rights that concern the common benefit and order, not inclusive of those of the individual or individual communities. The concept can be taken further to include the rights of all living and non-living things in the rights of God.

The right to life is also considered to be a right of God, and not a right of the individual. For that reason, the rights of God cannot be made subject to forgiveness nor can they be waived, as can other rights; such rights cannot be abolished or changed by humans or governments. Only God can forgive the trespasses against His rights.

The acts of terror that have been carried out in recent years, sometimes intended as a rebellion against modern values, sometimes in order to get opinions heard, along with individual or collective acts of suicide, are all outlawed by Islam. Whatever the reason may be, the individual has no right to act in such a manner. Some of these incidents stem from a misunderstanding or a misinterpretation of the religion, while others stem from a lack of a reliable and sound religious knowledge.

Still, the fact that such acts have become more common is an issue that must be examined. Whatever the aim of such an act, the reasons that lead a person to commit terrorism must be uncovered and eradicated; this is the foremost duty of humanity. Taking this situation lightly, turning a blind eye to it for petty reasons, or supporting those who cause such acts to be repeated must also be regarded as crimes against all of humanity.

On the other hand, it should not be ignored that narcissism and aggressive feelings play a large part in determining a person's behavior. When the emotion of "self-love," an emotion that enables the individual to protect themselves, is threatened in some way, the result is generally a state of shame or an injured consciousness, thus causing the individual to engage in aggressive action in order to reconstruct this emotion. Moreover, "ignorance," or insufficient and false knowledge, feeds bigotry, bigotry prepares the ground for fanaticism, and fanaticism leaves the door ajar to terror. When the field in which ignorance reigns is religion, the situation becomes even more complex. People who are not well informed about their own beliefs cannot formulate a healthy correlation between the values in which they believe and the life that they lead. Consequently, they lose connection with life and start to adopt illogical behavior, or they start to despise their values and develop inferiority complexes. Both are nothing but errant behavior.

As a matter of fact, terror is a consequence of desperate circumstances where no solutions can be developed. Desperate circumstances stem from ignorance, while helplessness derives from not possessing the necessary means. Individuals, thus societies, that are not equipped sufficiently in terms of education and intellectual wisdom produce problems rather than solutions and they are more likely to be abused by others. Moreover, problems arising from failure to fully utilize their available resources result in helplessness, and this helplessness gives rise to aggression.

The fact that the concept of jihad is invoked in acts of terror, acts which have gained popularity in the Islamic world due to various causes, like the ones given above, has made this concept a topic of discussion today.

Jihad

Etymologically, the word jihad has the meanings of effort, exertion, test, weathering, the extracting of butter from milk, or feeling hungry. In any struggle, force is activated and effort is exerted; it is in this way that jihad also comes to mean an active war. However it is interpreted, when all these different meanings are taken into consideration, four different dimensions of jihad arise:

a) The defensive dimension: This concept is usually associated with the terms *jihad*, *ghaza*, and *harb*. Although the word jihad and its conjugations are repeated some 34 times in the Qur'an, only four of these usages refer directly to war.[1] However, since most of the verses concerning jihad are found in passages that deal with the subject of war, this particular meaning has tended to gain the upper hand in interpretations.

b) The psychological dimension: Islamic thinkers, in particular Sufis, use the term *mujahada*, conjugated from the same root, in order to express the spiritual dimension of jihad—and this is addressed in three different categories: *mujahada* against the enemy is jihad; *mujahada* against the Devil is *taqwa*; and *mujahada* against the corporeal desires is *riyadha* (austerity). Ten verses concerning jihad in the Holy Qur'an deal with this last category.[2]

c) The intellectual dimension: This is expressed by the terms *ijtihad* (interpretation) and *tafakkur* (contemplation). *Ijtihad* means making a great effort to reach a difficult goal. Islamic jurists define the term *ijtihad* thus: The effort made by a jurist to arrive at a religious decree based on cases stemming from secondary suppositions. That is to say, the effort of a Muslim scholar to arrive at a decision using all his intellectual capabilities, both in religious affairs and non-religious affairs.[3]

d) The social dimension: This means serving the entire community and fighting against injustice. In this sense,

---

[1] Tawba 9:41, 73; Furqan 25:52; Tahrim 66:9.
[2] Hajj 22:78 ; Tawba 9:24, 88; Baqara 2:218; Al 'Imran 3:143; Hujurat 49:15; Ma'ida 5:35, 95; Ankabut 29:6; Mumtahana 60:1.
[3] Tawba 9:122.

the word jihad means to help people and struggle to prevent unfair actions.[4]

There are many hadith which are concerned with the psychological aspect of jihad. It was reported that after returning from a battle the Prophet said, "We have returned from the minor jihad to the major one."[5] Likewise, the Prophet said, "The *mujahid* is one who makes jihad against his/her own carnal self."[6] The following hadith makes clear the social aspect of this concept: "The messenger of God asked one of the Companions who wanted to participate in jihad (in the sense of war) whether his parents were alive. Upon receiving a positive answer, the Prophet told this man to make jihad for them (i.e., to serve them instead)."[7]

The Prophet once stated: "Those who work for widows and the poor are like those who make jihad for God."[8] Also, he declared that "It is the greatest jihad to speak words of justice and truth to an oppressive ruler."[9] Concerning the intellectual aspect of jihad, there are plenty of hadiths which promote contemplation, research and the attainment of both religious and non-religious knowledge.

As can be seen, in Islam the social, psychological, intellectual, and humane dimensions of jihad are more pronounced than the dimension that is related to war. In Islamic literature jihad does not necessarily denote war. The word has come to be used in place of war simply because communities spend all of their effort and power when they fight an enemy. In the Qur'an, it is seen that other words are used to directly denote war, such as *qital*, *harb*, *muharaba*, and *ma'raka*. As pointed out by the renowned Islamic scholar Muhammad Hamidullah, wars that are not in keeping with the goals that God has set are illegitimate in Islam. The wars that the Prophet engaged in were wars that were

---

[4] Ma'ida 5:54; Tawba 9:19; Anfal 8:72; Nahl 16:110; Ankabut 29:6, 8; Luqman 31:15.
[5] 'Ajluni 1/424.
[6] Tirmidhi, *Fada'il al-Jihad*, 2.
[7] Bukhari, *Jihad*, 138; Muslim, *Birr*, 5.
[8] Bukhari, *Nafaqa*, 1; Muslim, *Zuhd*, 41.
[9] Abu Dawud, *Malahim*, 17; Tirmidhi, *Fitan*, 13.

aimed at defense, punishing those who allied themselves with the enemy or betrayed the Muslim community by violating previous agreements, and the protection of Islamic lands (Hamidullah 1995, 222-223). It is for this reason that the aim of Islamic conquests has never been merely aggression, robbery, or plunder. Rather, the aim of such conflicts has always been to create an environment where people could freely choose the belief system that they wanted to follow. Consequently, Muslim conquerors let the people of other lands choose freely between becoming Muslim or living under Islamic rule levied with capitation tax (*jizya*), which is an alternative to *zakat* and *sadaqa*, taxes Muslim citizens are obliged to pay.

Islam has, from the very beginning, demanded that non-Muslims be well-treated in the lands where Muslims rule—whether these people were of the region and citizens of the conquered state or whether they were people who settled there later—in particular Christians and Jews, as they are considered to be People of the Book. It is reported that even with his last breath the Prophet advised his people to treat non-Muslims well. He is reported to have said that "those who ill-treat Christians and Jews will answer to me on Judgment Day"[10] and that "those who do injustice to Christians and Jews will not be able to enter Paradise."[11]

In Islam, fields and trees cannot be set on fire during wartime, nor can temples or buildings be destroyed. The killing of women, children, the elderly, the blind, and members of the clergy is forbidden. The taxes that are collected from the non-Muslim population cannot be used to meet the expenses of Muslims, but the alms collected from Muslims can be used to provide for non-Muslims who are in need.[12]

In the decree promulgated by Caliph 'Umar to Abu Musa al-Ashari when he was posted as governor of Basra, it is instructed

---

[10] 'Ajluni 2/285; Baghdadi 8/370.
[11] Darimi, *Seerah*, 16.
[12] Ibn Rushd 1/348.

that all who come to the governor should be treated equally, that all those who come to trials should be seated together in the courtroom and that the governor should even be equal in the looks that he dispenses to each side during a trial, with no discrimination of religious tradition: ". . . Thus the rich among them should not think that you will rule unjustly, nor the poor think that injustice will be inflicted upon them."[13]

Holy War and Just War in Christianity

In Christianity, which has manifested itself as a religion that is on the side of peace, the concept of war occupies a very important place. The Christians, who suffered greatly, especially during the Roman era, chose "passive resistance" as their way to put an end to Roman oppression, and overlooked the warring and fighting aspect of this religion; rather they attempted to highlight the aspects of peace and tolerance found within.

Starting with Marcion of Sinop, early Christian writers wanted to make sovereign not the "creating, judging, ruling, and punishing God Jehovah" of the Old Testament, but the "savior, the forgiving God of Love, Jesus Messiah."

According to Christian scriptures, the greatest order God has given is to love God and to love one's neighbor. Just as Jesus loved his disciples, he also preached that they should love one another.

As stated in the Gospels according to Matthew, Jesus said the following:

> But I say unto you, that you resist not evil: but whosoever shall smite you on your right cheek, turn to him the other also. And if any man will sue you at the law, and take away your coat, let him have [your] cloak also. (Matthew 5:39-40)

---

[13] Baykhaki, 10/150; Daraktuni, 4/206; Sarahsi, 16/61.

We see that alongside these messages of love, messages of war also occupy a great part of the New Testament.

> Think not that I am come to send peace on earth: I came not to send peace, but a sword. For I am come to set a man at variance against his father, and the daughter against her mother, and the daughter-in-law against her mother-in-law. (Matthew 10:34-35)

> Suppose you that I am come to give peace on earth? I tell you, Nay; but rather division. For from henceforth there shall be five in one house divided, three against two, and two against three. The father shall be divided against the son, and the son against the father; the mother against the daughter, and the daughter against the mother; the mother-in-law against her daughter-in-law, and the daughter-in-law against her mother-in-law. (Luke 12:51-53)

According to the Bible, acts of violence and catastrophes will befall toward the end of time to prepare the world for the second coming of Jesus, who *shall rule (them) with a rod of iron as the vessels of potter shall they be broken to shivers* (Revelation 2:27-28).

> And the fourth angel sounded, and the third part of the sun was smitten, and the third part of the moon, and the third part of the stars; so as the third part of them was darkened, and the day shone not for a third part of it, and the night likewise. (Revelation 8:12)

In surveys that have been carried out in the USA, it has been discovered that around 30% of the population with religious beliefs believe that the world will end with the wars of Armageddon. Fanatic groups have emerged, some of which have even committed mass suicide. For instance, Jim Jones, the leader of the People's Temple sect, in his sermons in 1978 preached that the world had come to an end and that this indicated the Armageddon mentioned in the Bible. He said "Judgment Day is at our footsteps, let us go with it and be the first in the crowd." As we all know, 913 people committed suicide pursuit of this goal. (Halsel 2002, 21) On the other hand, some Christian groups believe that the world has come or is coming to an end, and they feel they have to be near the Messiah and therefore go to Jerusalem to die. Professor François Mayer claims that since the 1850s many people have left the USA to go to Palestine for that very reason.

When people of different views were started to be oppressed—like Donatus and the Donatists who did not accept the Patriarch appointed by Constantine in the fourth century, and Arius, Makedonius, Nestorius and their followers—the pacifist character of Christianity was damaged.

In the fifth century, when the Barbarian hordes threatened Rome, the famous Christian saint Augustine argued that war could be legitimate for Christians under certain circumstances and he was the first to voice the concept of "a just war." In the thirteenth century, St. Thomas developed this concept and systemized it. According to him, to designate a war a "just war" the following three principles must be present:

1) The right to declare war resides with a legitimate authority.

2) It must be based on defense against aggression, or a legitimate cause like the protection of the rights of believers.

3) It must be aimed at the sovereignty of goodness and the eradication of evil.

Starting from the tenth century, with the recapture of Spain and the Crusades in Western Europe, a new concept entered Christian literature: that of "Holy War."

This concept connoted an argument that encouraged attack and legitimized war, according to the argument "God has enemies and these enemies want to destroy all those who submit themselves to God. The enemies of God are those who go against Christianity, the true religion of God and therefore they must be fought and destroyed."

In the fourteenth century, St. Raymond Lulle (of Spanish origin), a man who continuously slandered the jihad concept in Islam, said, "Missionaries who try to convert Muslims into Christianity should first of all take love as their principle. They have to use Jesus' way of loving all. Secondly, they have to let the Muslims choose Christianity with their own free will. But if they should resist after they have been told about Christianity, the true religion, then it would be legitimate to make them accept Christianity through the use of force" (Ramon 1983, 375).

The Crusades, which continued for more than 300 years, left bitter and unpleasant memories both in the Western societies that waged it and among the Muslims. For that reason, the term "Holy War" was set aside in Christianity to be replaced with the concept of "a just war"; this denoted a war of "good vs. evil."

With the French Revolution and the Enlightenment, the religious context of this concept was lost and it assumed a secular guise. According to this new guise, a "just war" was a war that did not have aggression as its aim; rather it was a defensive war. There must be a group of people who were rebelling against an oppressive government and who are, for that reason, faced with even greater oppression. Any intervention had to be carried out by a legitimate authority and had to be limited. This concept was first brought to discussion in modern times by Michael Walzer, who opposed America's Vietnam War, in terms of its legitimacy and ethical dimensions.

Perpetual Peace

The German philosopher Emmanuel Kant developed the term "Perpetual Peace" in place of "just war." In the treatise "Perpetual Peace," he wrote toward the end of his life, he addressed the theoretical, political, and legal aspects of the idea of "perpetual peace," and delved into how a world without war could be achieved. Kant speaks of 6 main principles for the institution of "perpetual peace" on Earth:

1) No treaty of peace shall be held valid in which there is tacitly reserved matter for a future war.

2) No independent states, large or small, shall come under the dominion of another state by inheritance, exchange, purchase, or donation.

3) Standing armies shall in time be totally abolished.

4) National debts shall not be contracted with a view to the external friction of states.

5) No state shall by force interfere with the constitution or government of another state.

6) No state shall, during war, permit such acts of hostility which would make mutual confidence in the subsequent peace impossible: such are the employment of assassins, poisoners, breach of capitulation, and incitement to treason in the opposing state.

According to Kant, for "perpetual peace" to be realized, everyone should assume responsibility, and values, such as "good intentions" and "duty ethics," must be cultivated; behind the state of peace and war lie ethical questions. The nature of humanity is the greatest assurance for the propagation of peace; it is not an obstacle in its path.

But it is a common fact that ethics and politics usually contradict one another. In order to alleviate this contradiction, "transcendentalism," which is the starting point of Kantian idealism, should be applied in the field of universal law.

Kant's ideal was attempted on a relatively large scale with the establishment of United Nations after the Second World War. But the situation that we have arrived at today gives the impression that we are back at how things were before the Second World War. The only way to put a halt to this course of events is to develop the concept of global ethics.

The Need for Global Ethics

The fact that the most basic problem that modern society is faced with today is not a political, social, or economic problem, but an ethical one, is now very clear. It is impossible for a society that lacks ethical pillars to remain standing. Leslie Lipson thinks in a similar way:

> Western civilization is now in need—like never before—of an ethical revolution that is in keeping with Humanism. Western society has succumbed to failure in the first half of this century and since then it has been crawling towards the edge of the precipice.
>
> Those who are to blame for this are the scientists who do not take responsibility for the ethical outcomes of their discoveries, the economists who claim that production for economic gain is unrelated to ethical principles, the political scientists who limit themselves to forms of technical methods and systems of governance, and all those others who do not distinguish between good and bad knowledge, thus turning a blind eye to the things that are most damaging to society.
>
> The West, suffering from giddiness due to its own material success, has allowed materialism and the commercial superiority that comes along with it, to rule over all else. Today, the worship of the Golden Calf[14] has been replaced by the worship of the idolized gross national product. But goals have to be sought elsewhere. They should be sought in humanism, good citizenship, and good society. In the history of all civilizations, at every point of human development, one can come across occurrences of evil. But we have introduced brand-new evils into the twentieth century. All these evils are connected with the irresponsible methods that we use when we apply technology to our daily use. The existence of nuclear weapons, the pollution of the environment and its out-right destruction, the population

---

[14] *So he brought forth for them a calf, a (mere) body, which had a mooing sound, so they said: This is your god and the god of Moses, but he forgot.* (Ta-Ha 20:88)

explosion in areas where living standards are already low—
these are such problems that if they are not solved the result will
be one of the two following scenarios: Either the quality of civilization in all parts of the world will decline, including that in
rich areas, or the planet itself will become an untenable place to
live.

Thus, the following question arises: What must we, all of
humanity, do in order to escape such an eventuality? In my
opinion, what we need are radical changes that will go down
deep to the roots of the civilization that we are familiar with.
Only a complete, radical attempt can save us from decline.
There are two requisites for this action: the first one will involve
a revolution in our institutions and the second, in our values. If
civilization is to be protected and to continue to rise, these two
requisites have to go hand in hand. (Lipson 2000, 298-300)

Francis Fukuyama, who has attracted interest with his "The
End of History?" thesis, argues that at the root of the development of societies and progress lies the feeling of trust, and that
social welfare cannot be instituted without such a feeling. The
institution of trust depends on the establishment of a strong civil
social structure. Civil society has a complex structure which is
comprised of firms, educational establishments, NGOs, the media, unions, charitable organizations, clubs, and religious institutions. Civil society is built upon the institution of the family,
which passes on the values and knowledge pertaining to that
society from generation to generation and provides for the qualities that enable individuals to live in a larger society. But a
strong, consistent family structure and social institutions that
have continuity do not come about through legislation, as do
governments, central banks, or national forces. A successful civil
society is built upon the habits, traditions, and ethical values of
the individual.

In socialization and in the furthering of social welfare the
main propagating force is culture. For that reason societies have

to make a great effort to maintain the cultural values which they have inherited from their past. Reasonable approaches and positive values cannot always be solutions by themselves alone; there must also be moral and spiritual values.

In the twenty-first century, there is a need for measures that will enhance trust among different societies. And this can only be achieved by bringing together traditional cultures with modern institutions in a viable synthesis. Economic activity in the modern world is carried out, not by individuals, but by organizations that require the utmost social cooperation. Right to possessions, contracts and trade laws are all essential institutions for forming an economic system with modern market tendencies. But such institutions are only significant when coupled with social capital and trust.

> It cannot be claimed that these social norms and rules are not modern. In order for modern democracy to be functional, rational values and ethical values have to co-exist. Law, contracts, and economic rationality are elements that are needed for the prosperity of post-industrial societies, but they are not enough. As well as these values that rest upon rationality, there have to be values that are based on habits, mutual relations, ethical responsibilities and duties, and trust within society. These values are not in any way out-dated. On the contrary, they are indispensable elements of the success of modern society. (Fukuyama 1998)

Our globalized world is in need more than ever of new global ethics that will be valid everywhere. It is imperative that the approach of "global ethics" that has been developed by Protestant intellectuals, such as Hans Küng and Josef Kushel, should be enriched, especially with the intellectual tradition of Islamic thinking.

References

Bukhari, *Sahih*; Muslim, *Sahih*; Tirmidhi, *Sunan*; Darimi, *Sunan*; Darakutni, *Sunan*; Ajluni, *Kashf al-Khafa*; Hatip al-Baghdadi, *Tarikh al-Baghdad*; Ibn Rushd, *Bidaya al-Mujtaid*.

The Holy Bible, King James Version. Matthew, Luke, Revelations.

Hamidullah, Muhammad. *Islam Anayasa Hukuku*, Istanbul: 1995. Originally published as *The First Written Constitution in the World*, Lahore: 1975.

al-Shatibi. *al-Muwafaqa fi usul al-shari'a*, Cairo: Al-Maktaba al-tijariyya al-kubra, 1975 4:60

Sarahsi, *Al-Mabsut*, Cairo.

Fukuyama, Francis. *Güven, Sosyal Erdemler ve Refahın Yaratılması*, Ankara: 1998. Translated by Ahmet Buğdaycı. Originally published as *Trust: The Social Virtues and the Creation of Prosperity*, Free Press, 1995.

Halsell, Grace. *Tanrıyı Kıyamete Zorlamak*. Translated by M. Acar- H. Ozmen, Ankara: 2002. Originally published as *Forcing God's Hands: Why Millions Pray for a Quick Rapture -- and Destruction of Planet Earth*, Washington, DC: Crossroads International Publishing, 1999.

Lipson, Leslie, *Uygarlığın Ahlaki Bunalımları*, Istanbul: 2000. Translated by Jale Yeşilbaş. Originally published as *The Ethical Crises of Civilization: Moral Meltdown or Advance?* Sage Publications, 1993.

Ramon Sugranyes de Franch. *L'Apologetique de Raimond Lulle vis-a-vis de l'Islam*, Toulouse: Cahier de Fanjeaux, XVIII, 1983.

JIHAD

Ali Bulaç

The Modern Development of the Concept of Jihad

If we want to have a correct overall idea of what the actions and behavior of Muslims can signify, there are primarily three things that must be taken into consideration: the first of these are the Qur'an and the Sunna (that is, the sayings of our Prophet, his actions, and actions of which he approved) which provide the framework of legitimacy for all Muslim individuals. Secondly, the traditional and cultural structures that Muslims have developed throughout their history; and thirdly, the ideas and views that an outsider may hold, which change according to the level of knowledge and the observation of the observer. Generally, the difference between these three basic factors is not taken into consideration, therefore making it difficult to determine what actually springs from the original nature of the religion, what is the result of the limited understanding of those who practice the religion and the impact of their historical situation, or lastly, what is caused by careless observation and insufficient knowledge that have led to the formulation of prejudices. In recent history, with wars of independence taking place against colonialism in 80% of the occupied Islamic world, the term jihad has activated a magnificent human energy which had formerly been dormant; Islamic scholars and leaders who were quick to grasp the possible consequences of this energy declared jihad as being something that can be employed against colonialism. In the Caucasus, in India, and in the colonized Middle East, as the struggle against the occupying forces gained ground, jihad was used as a defense mechanism and as a framework that established the legitimacy of war. Naturally, the jihad movement was directed against "Western forces," who were the "occupying power" whose negative definition in religious and political literature led to a figure of the "other"; a figure that had to be fought against. This, in turn, led to a strong prejudice in the West against jihad, where there was already a particular view of Muslims that had been created by historical relations.

As the first Islamist generations of the nineteenth century formulated the project of Islamism as an intellectual and political movement, they opened the way for *ijtihad*[1] by returning to the Qur'an and the original sources of the religion, and in so doing, they placed a special emphasis on jihad and the awakening of a spirit of jihad. But what was understood from jihad was redefined in a new conceptual frame as resistance against colonialism: the term jihad was to be used pragmatically for the procuring of the religious motivation which was needed for economic, scientific and technological progress. Yet another meaning of jihad occurred when placed within a new definition; the eradication of the sloth that had taken root in the society for a long time, and the start of a movement that was directed toward an intellectual, social, and material awakening. Just as water stagnates when still, so too does social life fall into lethargy when it stops moving. Jihad was taken as a spiritual source that called into action a spiritual energy, a transforming and propagating force for the new communal movement and the shaking off of the old colonialism; dynamic social projects were produced based on this energy.

Despite all their painstaking efforts, Western orientalists and researchers did not take this extremely important development, one that pertains to modern times and modernizes the concept of jihad, into consideration. They considered jihad to be religious dissemination that threatened civilization, something akin to the

---

[1] *Ijtihad*: (Literally, utmost effort). The exercise of reason in order to try to find an appropriate ruling on a matter not directly related upon in the Qur'an.

Christian concept of crusade, i.e., terror as a means of realizing a particular political aim or blind fanaticism spurred on by religious fervor. (Peters, 1989)

The Place of Jihad in Basic Islamic Terminology

Islam, which accepts other religious traditions, such as Judaism and Christianity, as being holy messages that have been revealed before its advent, has some "key terms" in its theological frame of existence, knowledge, and morals. These key terms, which also make up the basis of the Islamic faith, consist of *Tawhid* (belief in the absolute unity of God), *Risala* (God communicating with humanity through a messenger), *Akhira* (eternal life after death) and a few related terms. Even though jihad is not one of the pillars of faith, it is still one of the key terms which help us to understand the individual and social aspects of Islam. The military and political battles that Muslims fought with non-Muslims throughout history have led to some semantic differences in the concept of jihad, just as with some other concepts. Here, it is possible to say that historical movements and mode of government have played a crucial role. For example, the term *sadaqa* (alms) is in fact connected to the word *tasadduq* (giving alms), and therefore it can express the idea of "voluntary financial help" or "obligatory state tax" at one and the same time; in fact, its meaning has been transformed today into a mere pittance given to the poor and beggars on a voluntary basis.

Likewise, the term jihad has changed in meaning and has come to mean war that is waged for the sake of belief and the resulting military expansion and conquest of lands, diverging from the meaning employed in the primary texts of religion that are binding and from the way that the Muslims of the first period understood it. But in truth, jihad has a broader meaning, spanning other concepts and meanings, much in the same way as the term *infaq* (giving one's possessions away) does. *Infaq*, as a term, covers all of the following concepts: *sadaqa* (voluntary or obligatory financial help, i.e., alms), *zakat* (a tax and/or *tasadduq* that Muslims have to pay, due from possession of gold, silver and commercial goods, and livestock, minerals and the like), *oshur*, which falls within the scope of *zakat* (a tax of 1/10 - 1/20 the value of agricultural products), *kharaj* (tax taken from those who cultivate land belonging to the state), *khumus* (a tax of 1/5 the value of mined minerals and metals)—all of these and similar concepts which are concerned with state taxation fall under the greater umbrella of *infaq* and each has a special meaning pertaining to an economic, industrial, or commercial field of activity. Considering jihad from one aspect of its diverse meanings, we can see that it accommodates other concepts, such as *qital* (battle), *muharaba* (war in action), *isyan* (rebellion), *jadal* (strife). Moreover, Arabic semantics are rich enough to express each action and attitude with a different word. *Qital* means actual fighting while *muharaba* is a state of war between two groups. Had jihad been simply "killing" and "war," then there would have been no need for the use of words like *qital* and *muharaba* in the Qur'an.

The Framework of the Definition

If we try to define jihad with respect to the structure of its true meaning, we could say the following: "Jihad is the effort made to remove obstacles that stand between humanity and God."

In this definition, humanity, God, and obstacles are all key terms. In the final analysis, humanity denotes the individual. The individual is the product of his or her belief, history, and socio-cultural environment. But if one so desires, one can free oneself from being enslaved to false beliefs, history, and environment, liberating oneself from being blown around like a leaf in the winds of circumstance. Islam is the final religion to be revealed by God, and it was revealed through the prophethood of Muhammad, peace be upon him. Obstacles, on the other hand, exist over a very broad area that ranges from the inner passions of the individual to the restrictions imposed upon one's freedom of

religion and conscience, to political oppression and social de-
pravity.

Consequently, it is possible to speak of two basic dimensions of jihad, a word that derives from the root *jahd*, which
means effort or struggle. The first of these is the spiritual and
moral effort that must be exerted to alleviate the restrictions and
obstacles that stem from the inner world of the individual and
their essential nature; the second is the sum total of all activity
that one has to engage in in order to make possible a physical and
social environment where religious life can be freely communi-
cated and practiced. In both cases, the individual has to put their
utmost efforts into this struggle to liberate humanity in both the
inner and the outer world.

"Islam," which is the goal of the religious life and the actions of the individual, means—beyond its concrete framework
of theology and law—submission to God, peace, salvation,
safety, and well-being. These concepts are the common denomi-
nators of almost all religions, and thus the Qur'an, referring to
the prophet Abraham as the common ancestor of all three monotheistic religions, calls him a "Muslim." By calling him a "Muslim,"[2] what is meant is that he was a prophet who submitted to
the will of God, who taught inner spiritual calm and peace in the
outside world; he was a chosen prophet who showed the practical
ways of instituting a social life where peace rules. Submission to
God requires living in *silm*. *Silm* means living in peace with God,
nature, other people, and with one's own self.

The Qur'an also reminds us that in truth religion is "unique
and one" and that there are only differences in the secondary and
tertiary rules in religious law; these differences have occurred in
accordance with historical circumstances, within the unchanging
basic principles of religion. This alludes to the fact that at the
root of submission to God lies the unity of existence, humanity,
and history. Thus, in the messages of all prophets and messen-

---

[2] "Muslim" derives from the same root with Islam, "*s-l-m*," which means submission and
peace.

gers, from the first to the last, one can see a continuous change concerning the secondary issues—but these changes never touch the core of the message and always remain secondary.

The fact that jihad is derived from the term *jahd* also indicates the relationship of this word to the word *ijtihad*, which is derived from the same root. The meaning of *ijtihad* is that a person who is intellectually and scientifically equipped exerts the utmost effort to derive judgments from passages in the Qur'an and the Sunna. The *jahd* which is carried out in this case with a particular *asl* (legitimate and trustworthy source, i.e. the Qur'an and the Sunna) and a particular *usul* (method) indicates scientific and intellectual effort. *Mujahada*, which is derived from the same root, relates more to the individual effort of a person for spiritual maturation and moral cleansing concerning the self (*mujahada* with the carnal self). If we accept *ijtihad* as being a dimension and methodology of scholarly effort, intellectual activity, and, in particular, law (Islamic jurisprudence or *fiqh*), we can also regard *mujahada* as being a method and way of Sufism as well.

The etymological richness of the word jihad demonstrates well the richness of human situations in which our life experiences manifest themselves. Undoubtedly, life is not composed solely of struggles and fights. Yet, we must always keep in mind that the forces of anger and desire contained within us can lead us astray in what seem to be legitimate circumstances; we must always be prepared for such an eventuality. What is essential is to keep these two forces under the control of the mind, which is illuminated by the divine light of the heart, i.e., the force of the intellect, in a way that will direct these forces towards legitimate and beneficial goals. This is the greatest struggle and the *mujahada*.

The basic dimension of jihad that concerns the inner life of the individual expresses the struggle against the will and desires of the *nafs* (carnal self); *nafs* is a basic concept found in Islamic literature, its ontological root meaning "thick darkness." What it signifies is a love for the material world and extreme dependence on the worldly nature of our essential being. Ambition, selfishness, sensuality, addiction to bodily desires, pursuit of material pleasures, adoration of the world, and exalting worldly values and desires so that they become like a fetish are the primary characteristics of the *nafs*.

Humanity has a concentric dual nature. The first part of this nature is the worldly nature and the other is the spiritual/soulful nature. The home of this second nature is the heart, and the home of the worldly nature is our bodily desires and passions (our *nafs*). The goal of the creation of humanity is, uniquely, to put the spiritual nature above the worldly nature. The freedom which is to be gained through *jahd* and *mujahada* is the attainment of the power to consciously regulate our worldly nature and to hold onto this power. God Himself created humankind with His "hands"[3] in the best form and nature; He has breathed into us of His Spirit, taught us the names (i.e., the knowledge of all that exists), and shown us the way, through His messengers. The aim of creation is that we are servants to God in the best possible way; the route to this perfection or the result of attaining this level is transformation into *insan al-kamil*, a perfect and mature human being, a person who possesses the highest degree of moral and spiritual maturity. The divine essence that is present in humanity calls us to God and Heaven; this is where people actually belong; worldly nature, which is the field of existence for *nafs*, on the other hand, calls humans to the Earth and the mud. Humanity is the fruit of the tree of existence, the most perfect creation; if we so desire, with the leave, help, and power of God, we can fight against the evil that the *nafs* encourages in us and

---

[3] *O Iblis! What prevented you from prostrating yourself to one whom I have created with My Own Hands?* (Sad 38:75). God is beyond any physical or human attributes. The Arabic word *yad* (hand) used in this verse and others in the Qur'an always assumes a meaning of exaltation when associated with God. According to many commentators, this verse underlines the significance of humankind in terms of its creation and position above other creatures.

we can realize the goal of creation. Another name for this struggle is *mujahada*, i.e., jihad.

According to Islam, this great spiritual effort is understood as the major jihad. According to what has been reported, the Prophet, peace and blessings be upon him, after returning from the Battle of Badr said to his victorious friends: "You have now returned from the minor jihad to the major one." When he was asked "What is the major jihad?" he replied: "It is jihad against the *nafs*."[4] He is also reported to have said, "Real *mujahids* are those who fight against their *nafs*."[5]

This inner dimension of jihad is vitally important. People who have not fought against the evil inherent in their nature, people who have failed to overcome the obstacles standing in the way of spiritual and moral maturation cannot be expected to make a fruitful, successful effort to lead others in the outside world toward the true path. In this frame of understanding, jihad means the maximum struggle that the individual engages in on route to spiritual cleansing; the control of the *nafs* and disciplining oneself with respect to moral virtues. Since this is the most difficult of all struggles, it is considered that "Jihad against the *nafs* is the greatest jihad."

The Law, War, and Jihad

As far as the surface meaning of jihad is concerned, there is a widespread view that Muslims sanctify war in order to compel people of other religions to "convert to Islam," or that jihad has been politicized, with violence and terror against others being employed for their own ends, with legitimacy taken from Islam. The Western media sometimes even shows violence and terror that are politically aimed as being so-called examples of modern "Islamic jihad."

Here, the best way to avoid confusion is to make a distinction between war, which is—as stated at the beginning of the

---

[4] 'Ajluni, *Kashf al-Khafa*, 1/45.
[5] Tirmidhi, *Fada'il al-Jihad*, 2.

article—a topic of international law that is currently on the agenda in international relations, (that is, say actual fighting) and jihad, with its much broader semantics. One of the aspects of jihad is undoubtedly war. When listing the four classical and natural functions of the state, the Hanafi jurists (Hanafi being one of the great Islamic schools of thought)—by consensus—include jihad. According to them, the four basic duties of a state are as follows: sovereignty and representation of sovereignty (the practice of public Friday prayer); the collection of taxes and the spending of the same on shared and indivisible services (*fay*), protection of domestic security and the independence of jurisdiction (the authority to sentence), and the defense of the country (the proclamation of jihad). Hanafi jurists consider defense to fall under the authority of the state under the title of "jihad." This does not mean continuous struggle, as in the Marxist system, or a Nazi-like view which adopts "struggle until the entire world accepts the superiority of a particular race"; on the contrary, this administrative authority demonstrates that all issues must be considered within the scope of law. The fact that this duty is imposed on the state emphasizes that the authority for declaring war against another country and thereby engaging in jihad can only rest in the hands of a legitimate public authority; individuals, civil groups, communities, or political groups cannot, on their own, declare war under the name of jihad.

Despite this clear fact that has been determined by law, Hans Kruse defines jihad as "a continuous war between the Islamic community and non-Muslims." It is not clear whether he has arrived at this conclusion by studying historical examples or whether he bases it on the fundamental sources of the religion. In truth, when reliable sources are consulted, no "continuous jihad" that has the meaning of *qital* or war can be found; it is not an obligatory (*fard*) duty that all Muslims must perform. The borders of an Islamic country are to be protected by armed forces, that is to say the official military of the country. The first jurists among the Companions of the Prophet, 'Abd 'Allah ibn 'Umar,

'Amr ibn Dinar and Sufyan al-Sawri were all of this conviction. According to these jurists and scholars, if the borders of the Islamic land are safe, war loses its necessity; it is no longer obligatory (Abu Suleiman, 1985, p. 24).

The connection of jihad with war can be found by focusing on fighting in a spiritual way for the maturation of the character, and expecting reward only from God. People who are struggling in this way will fight in wars of legitimate and just causes, giving their lives for the freedom and independence of people because this act is approved of by God as an exalted cause. A person who dies when defending their faith, wealth, honor, mental or physical health, or life is considered to be a "martyr." Jihad is not, as the orientalist Joseph Schact suggests, "a Holy War which expands the *Dar al-Islam* (lands of Islam) against the *Dar al-Harb* (non-Islamic lands) and which guarantees that this will go on until the whole world is converted to Islam and falls under Islamic sovereignty." (Schact 1997, p. 139) We should point out here that the concept of Holy War is completely a Western concept and, as with so many other issues, rather than treating jihad within its true meaning and place in Islam, some Western intellectuals have tried to place jihad within their own system of concepts and understanding, and thus have tended to translate jihad as meaning Holy War. Moreover, Schact evidently confuses "Holy War" with the military wars that result due to disputes between states. As stated just above, "Holy War" is a concept which is foreign to the political and military understanding of Muslims. War, undesirable as it may be, is a different form of politics. Jihad, in this particular sense, can only be carried out by the power of the state, i.e., the legitimate public authority. The aim of such a war would be to obtain a just and deserved result, and such a war must be executed within the limits of legitimacy. Rumi said, "War was made obligatory so that the swords are taken out of the hands of the oppressors." Moreover, Islamic law would never use the adjective "holy" for war; on the contrary, in the Qur'an it is stated that war always seems evil to humanity

(Baqara 2:216) and therefore it is limited in Islam so that the end result may lead to better ways. There is no claim in Islam to make the entire world Muslim. The Qur'an clearly says that *Not all people will believe (like Muslims)* (Yusuf 12:106) An individual can only find the right path and attain salvation (*hidaya*) through the will of God (*mashia*) and through His guidance. Even though personal effort is very important and necessary, faith is a divine privilege. This being so, it is unthinkable that someone should be made to find *hidaya* or enter the faith by force. The Qur'an speaks to the Prophet, and thus to all believers, in the following manner. *Remind them, for you are only a reminder. You are not a watcher over them* (Ghashiya 88:21-22). The most basic principle is the following:

> There is no coercion in (the choice of) religion. (Baqara 2:256)

On the contrary, one of the legitimate causes of war is the institution of freedom of religion and conscience and the alleviation of the obstacles that lay between the conscience of the individual and God. If, as human beings, we have a responsibility on this front, then it is the responsibility to alleviate these obstacles. But, if a state has guaranteed freedom of religion and conscience under the laws and constitution within the supremacy of law, there then will be no pressure on the people to choose a certain religion. Oppressive regimes not only obstruct freedom of religion, conscience, and expression, but they also create a multitude of injustices and moral degeneration. To struggle for freedom and justice against such an oppressive regime is one of the moral goals of jihad. Prophet Muhammad, peace be upon him, said the following to make clear the legitimate aims of internal politics:

> It is the greatest jihad to speak words of justice and truth to an oppressive ruler.[6]

---

[6] Abu Dawud, *Malahim*, 17.

A guarantee of freedom of religion and conscience, possessing the right to live the way in which one desires, and the institution of justice in a way from which everyone can profit are norms from which not only Muslims are privileged to benefit, but also non-Muslims can benefit. As a principle, the existence of more than one religion, more than one belief, one way of thinking and living determines the general framework of pluralism. God does not wish all people to be exactly the same, as if they were produced from exactly the same mold. There are ontological differences, allowing us to see which community fares better than others. Undoubtedly, there will be theological and epistemological discussions between different religions. But these should not be made into grounds for war and battle. God will judge the issues upon which people and communities debate among themselves. In this world, what falls upon us is to compete amongst ourselves for the attainment of all that is true and beautiful.

But it is inevitable that humanity, which has, along with our virtues, a greedy, selfish, domineering and destructive nature, will not always abide by moral principles, will covet what we have no right to, will violate the rights of others. The cause of a legitimate and just war can only exist in such situations. Apart from wars of defense and offensive wars against those who have evil designs, it is also possible to declare war for the establishment of freedom of religion and conscience, and for the establishment of basic rights and liberties. A world free from arms and the threat of war is a world greatly desired; a wonderful ideal. But the facts of history and everyday life demonstrate that we are very far from that ideal. Consequently, we have to live with this continuous threat. If this is the case, then at least we have to base war on moral and just foundations. Islam has accepted the fact of war, not as a principle duty, but as a circumstantial and inescapable eventuality.

The institution of the freedom of religion and conscience, and the protection of places of worship has been addressed in the Qur'an as well:

> Those who have been expelled from their homes without a just
> cause except that they say: "Our Lord is God." And had there
> not been God's repelling some people by others, certainly there
> would have been pulled down cloisters and churches and syna-
> gogues and mosques in which God's name is much remem-
> bered. (Hajj 22:40)

The verb *def'*, (repel) in this verse is derived from the root *d-f-'a,* one of the meanings of which is war. But it is not possible to limit the meaning of jihad in the sense of actual combat (*mu-qatala*). Since the verb principally means "to get rid of," there is a meaning of resistance against all sorts of political and ideological pressure. To engage in political and legal struggle to ensure the freedom of religion and conscience in a country, to strive for the alleviation of pressure imposed on people, to make an intellectual effort in this, to develop civil reaction, to form platforms to that end, to participate in such platforms and to be a member of such all fall under the meaning of the forms of *def'*.

How can a religion which calls for action (even at the risk of war) against the alleviation of pressure for even non-Muslims be seen to be the legitimate cause of forcefully making people convert to Islam or of violence and terror directed against innocent people?

In history, there are instances that demonstrate Islam's attention to the rights of non-Muslims. After the conclusion of a bloody war with the Mongolians, the Muslims laid down the condition that non-Muslim slaves were to be freed as well. This was so unusual a situation that the Mongolian commander, Kutlu Shah, asked Ibn Taymiya, the spokesman and negotiator for the Muslims: "What do you mean to say? That you will continue to fight if we do not set free the Christian and Jewish slaves?" Ibn Taymiya said "Yes, that is exactly what we mean." According to Ibn Taymiya, to ensure the freedom of non-Muslims with whom the Muslims have made pacts, Muslims must fight; this is jihad for the sake of God.[7]

> So when the sacred months have passed away, then slay the pagans wherever you find them, and take them captives and besiege them and lie in wait for them in every ambush, then if they repent and keep up prayer and pay the poor-rate, leave their way free to them; surely God is Forgiving, Merciful. (Tawba 9:5)

This verse, as explained in the first four verses of the same chapter (Tawba), is talking about a condition when all possibilities of agreement and treaty have been exhausted, when all diplomatic relations have been sundered and when the eventuality of war is present. In the fourth verse it is stated:

> Do not kill those of the pagans with whom you made an agreement, then they have not failed you in anything and have not backed up with any one against you. (Tawba 9:4)

In the sixth verse, it is ordered that the pagans who seek refuge or protection should be excluded from the fighting. In short, these verses apply only to an actual state of war.

Here we have to make clear on what grounds war is considered to be in existence, both with regards to theory of war and to religion. As stated at the beginning, war is a state of military combat that results from political differences and disputes; this has a "secular" nature. The Prussian General Clausewitz defined war as "the continuation of politics with different tools." War is a method that can be exploited in order to make people accept a political aim with the use of force.

According to the majority of Islamic jurists (*jumhur*), the causality principle (*illat*) of war in Islam is an enemy attack on

---

[7] Abu Zahra, *Imam Ibn Taymiyya*, Istanbul: İslamoğlu Yayınları.

Islam and the land of the Muslims.[8] The cause for war is defined in the following verse:

> And fight in the way of God with those who fight with you, and
> do not exceed the limits, surely God does not love those who
> exceed the limits. (Baqara 2:190)

In other words the causality principle of war is not to make non-Muslims convert into Islam. If it were so, all non-Muslim people would have to be fought against and killed, without making distinctions between male-female, child-adult, clergy-civilian; but to do so would be "to exceed the limits," which is prohibited in the verse. But the fact is, even if there is a state of actual war with the enemy, Muslims cannot kill women, children, the elderly, the disabled, the clergy, or even civilian men who are taking no active part in the war.

Even if the enemy should not abide with the general moral norms and legal rules stated above, Islamic law does not, even then, permit the practice of an eye for an eye. That is to say, if Muslim women have been raped in the war, the Muslim soldiers must not retaliate by raping the women of the enemy (Abu Zahra 1976, 42). Therefore, in Islam, the rape of women has been a "war crime" since the Qur'an was first revealed in the seventh century. But in the modern world, this act has only been accepted as a war crime in 2001. In 1994, seven years after Serbian soldiers had raped some fifty thousand Muslim women and girls, three Serbian soldiers were found guilty and sentenced to prison at the tribunal set up in The Hague. Only after this tribunal, the international community accepted the rape of women by enemy soldiers as being a "war crime." These legal rules concerning war were set down clearly by the Prophet centuries ago, and Muslims have been instructed to abide by them up until the present time. (For further reference, see Yaman 1998, p. 57.)

---

[8] Sarahsi, *al Mabsut*, 10/5.

Taking into consideration the basic decrees and binding legal rules concerning legitimate warfare as stated above, how can one then consider jihad and terror (which aims at the ending of the lives of innocent people and is, in the final analysis, a crime against humanity) as being the same thing?

When closely examined, according to the framework envisaged by Islam, the foundations of the relations between religions have to be established on mutual respect and the acceptance; the sacred space of each, with their particular way of belief, and the right to worship should be considered as being protected from all kinds of violation and attack. This principle of mutual respect will encourage religions to "compete (to try to achieve more) in *khayr* (good deeds)."

Khayr semantically is a broad concept. It contains basic values, such as beauty, morality, righteousness, and goodness. It calls for the institution of dialogue, cooperation, mutual help, tolerance, and concerted efforts to reach this goal. The situation at which we have arrived today makes it imperative that we underline not the disputes amongst religions, but rather the shared feeling of responsibility in the face of common problems and with equal cooperation.

References

Abu Sulayman. *İslam'ın Uluslararası İlişkiler Kuramı*, Istanbul: 1985. Translated by Fehmi Koru. Originally published as *The Theory of International Relations in Islam*.

Abu Zahra, Muhammad. *İslam'da Savaş Kavramı*, Istanbul: 1976, Translated by C. Karaağaçlı.

——. *Imam Ibn Taymiyya*, Istanbul: İslamoğlu Yayınları.

Peters, Rodolph. *İslam ve Sömürgecilik—Modern Zamanlarda Cihad Öğretisi*, Istanbul: 1989. Translated by S. Gündüz. Originally published as *Islam and Colonialism: The Doctrine of Jihad in Modern History*.

Schact, Joseph. İslam Hukukuna Giriş, Ankara: 1977. Translated by M. Dağ and A. Kadir Şener. Originally published as *A History of Islamic Legal Theories: An Introduction to Sunni Usul Al-Fiqh.*

Yaman, Ahmet. *İslam Devletler Hukukuna Giriş*, Istanbul: 1998.

TERROR AND CHEMICAL WEAPONS LEADING TO TERROR

Nevzat Tarhan

"WHO (the World Health Organization) allocated $110,000,000 dollars to exterminate a peculiar kind of plant growing on Sri Lanka; youngsters who chewed on this plant lost their sense of fear of death and were easily able to commit suicide. Necessary measures are being taken to reduce the risk of this plant spreading around the world." This was an interesting piece of news announced by news agencies in 2003.

The conclusion that Fluocsetine (Prozac), once known as the medicine of happiness, triggered a tendency to suicide in some patients, created a storm in psychiatry. And last year, one of the strongest anti-depressants, Parocsetine (Serotat), was banned in England as it was found to have similar suicidal effects; its abuse by young people was already a matter of debate among professionals.

All these developments raised the question of "are we facing a new danger?" among those involved in the psycho-pharmacological sciences. Have we enabled people with medical treatment to have the courage to kill themselves? Does this mean that a person who is on such medicines becomes little more than a robot? Or, even more frightening, has psychopharmacology become a science that is likely to be abused in acts of terrorism?

These developments suggest that it would not be difficult to turn a group of people into suicide attackers; one would have to train them in a training program that resembles a boot camp, and then give them medication that triggers a sense of euphoria, and then another dose of a different drug that will help them overcome the fear of death.

When the terrorist acts that have occurred over recent years, such as the attack of September 11th, and the attacks in the Middle East, are looked at from this perspective, the argument that terrorism is systematic and consists of organized events supported by powerful organizations gains more ground.

Soldier's Illness

During the American Civil War (1861-1865), and the Franco-Prussian War (1870-1871) morphine, administered by injection, was widely used among soldiers as a painkiller. It was used to help soldiers withstand pain from their wounds, injuries, and burns, and to help them to relax. However, when these soldiers were discharged from the hospital, they suffered from headaches, trembling, nausea, vomiting, and cramps. This clinical phenomenon came to be known as "soldier's illness." Later on, it was discovered that this was the result of the soldiers going through withdrawal; soldiers who had been previously treated with morphine experienced withdrawal symptoms when cut off from their morphine supply.

The Discovery of Opium

The hydrochloride salt of opium is found in a solution obtained from the stem of the opium plant; it is obtained by pricking the plant. It was generally smoked in a pipe, or chewed and swallowed in Europe and the Far East, and was a common drug used by the nobility. In 1804, a French chemist Seguin succeeded in obtaining colorless crystals of refined morphine from opium. And in 1812, another chemist from Germany, Serturner analyzed the substance scientifically and published his analysis as "The Analysis of Opium." It took a great deal of effort to transform morphine into an injection, but this was finally achieved in 1853.

The name of this substance, which was advertised as the miracle medicine, the medicine of happiness, and which was used both as an analgesic and a sedative, was taken from the name of the Greek mythological god of sleep and dreams, Morpheus. When one used morphine it was considered that one had let one's self go in the arms of this god. This habit was so common that some wealthy people would carry morphine in syringes, wrapped in silk handkerchiefs, always ready for an injection under the skin at any time they pleased. Pichan drew attention to the addictive effects morphine caused in his renowned book *Morphinisme* in 1890. In Turkey, Mazhar Osman published similar information in his book *Keyif Veren Zehirler* [Pleasure-giving Poisons] in 1934. Throughout the world, the addiction was more common among people in the health profession. Finally, once its adverse effects had been established, its use on soldiers as a method of pain relief during wartime was abandoned.

It would not be wrong to argue that today "Ecstasy" has begun to hold the place that morphine used to hold in society.

Are There Contemporary Suicide Medicines?

Psychedelic drugs, i.e., those drugs which make the spiritual side of human life apparent and visible, were initially defined as consisting of LSD and Mescaline in 1954, and later became influential in modern art and music.

Substances that have sedative and psychic effects, such as Mescaline, which is found in the Peyote Cacti in South America, were used in Aztec rituals. American Indians and Aztecs, who ate the leaves of the cacti and became ecstatic, called this plant the "Divine Plant." In 1895 the original molecule of Mescaline was identified. After the 1940s, by employing a similar pharmacology, LSD (an alkaloid of the ergot of rye) and psilocybin were also found. The Aztec mushroom was reproduced in clinical studies. Mescaline and other LSD-group substances produce feelings of excessive joy, and an excessive distortion of distance and depth perception. The person under the influence of these drugs talks incessantly about the past and the future. These substances stimulate religious feelings and a sense of strength, and all other things the person has suppressed at a subconscious level are poured out. While it is possible for alcoholics to have self-control to some degree, those who are under the influence of psychedelic drugs reveal everything, indiscriminately.

It is for this reason that some secret agencies, such as the CIA, used this substance in some major projects during the 1960s. Eventually such usage was outlawed.

LSD as a Drug used for Brain Washing

LSD was discovered on April 19, 1943, by Dr. Markus Hopmann in his laboratory; he realized that this substance had caused something strange to happen to him. Hopmann recorded all of the changes that LSD was causing him to go through, minute by minute. LSD was produced from an alkaloid of ergot of rye.

LSD was utilized by spies, secret services, and criminal organizations to access the minds of the "enemy," and, if necessary, to change those thoughts, between the years 1950 and 1966. With the adoption of the Helsinki Convention in 1964, such experiments on humans were banned, and thus these activities have officially ceased to happen.

The exposition of people to these kinds of substances, effected by spiking their food or drink and the subsequent monitoring of their behavior to attain data is not scientifically acceptable. But the same methods can be employed in order to brainwash people in a camp-like environment; drugs and inculcation make a powerful team. It would even be possible to direct people to specific targets and to turn them into suicide bombers.

There are other substances that could be used by relevant groups to gain the loyalty of their members; this would help force the "soldiers" to perform the desired actions. If people can be groomed to be suicide attackers by providing them with drugs that boost their courage and with other substances that eliminate their fear of death, then the most expensive rockets would become obsolete.

Drugs That Boost Courage and Eliminate Fear of Death

"Ecstasy" is an illegal synthetic substance, and it is scientifically known as MDMA (metile endioxy metame fetamine). It is also called the "club drug" because it is used widely in night clubs, as it provides an artificial feeling of joy. The content of Ecstasy, which is produced illegally, is enriched with caffeine, "syrup of immortality," and cocaine, to make what is commonly known as "speed." Amphetamines can keep people hyperactive and vigorous for hours. They increase the attention span enormously, making people feel strong and energetic. Unlike LSD, amphetamines do not distort the sense of reality. They exhaust the serotonin resource in the brain, which is the part of the brain that is related to the sense of happiness (NIDA 2004). The high self-esteem and uncontrolled courage that come with amphetamines give a person a feeling of being as if in another world. In order to be able to maintain such energy, the person craves the drug more and more. If a person harbors feelings of revenge and hatred, then such drugs bring these feelings up to the surface, and direct the person to the target, even if to go toward this target would be suicidal. Today, studies are underway in the field of psychopharmacology that look in how to stimulate the area of the brain that is responsible for conditions that are associated with panic and the fear of death.

Conclusion

A thousand years ago, a group known as the notorious "*Hash-hashiyyun*" (people of the poppies) terrorized the Muslim leaders, scholars, and Islamic governments in the Muslim world; they went to their death fearlessly; this was due to the poppies that they consumed. Today, however, it is possible to brainwash people with the help of modern chemical agents, and to direct the same people to carry out specific actions.

It is possible for any service, organization, or state that possesses chemical laboratories equipped with high technology to delve into the thoughts of a group of people with LSD; it is then possible to feed the same people new propaganda; propaganda that is aimed at certain targets. These people will then be directed—by making them imbibe Ecstasy or amphetamines—to do any action within the following 8 to 10 hours.

The sad part of this is that world peace is being put at risk, or perhaps it is even being destroyed by the hand of science.

References

Smith, K.M., Larivell Romanalli. *Club Drugs, Menthrlere Dioxymethamphetamire, Flunitrazapam, Ketamire Hydrochloride and Gamma Hidroxybutyrtae*, I. Health, Syst., 2002, Pharm, 59, 1067-1076.

NIDA Forteens. "Fact on Drugs-Ecstasy," www.teensdrugabuse. gov.2004.

Dugiero G.Schifanorf, Forza G. *Personality Dimensions and Psychopathological Profiles of Ecstasy Users*, Hum Psychopharmalogical Clin Exp, 2001, 16/635-639.

Köknel Ö. *Alkolden Eroine Kişilikten Kaçış*, Istanbul: Altın Kitaplar, 1983.

Tarhan, N. *Psikolojik Savaş*, Istanbul: Timaş Yayınevi, 2002.

F. al-Syed, "The Neurochemistry of Drugs of Abuse, Cocaine, Ibagaine, and Substituted Amphetamines," *Annals of the New York Academy Sciences*, 1989, Vol. 844.

Harvery J. and B. Kosofsky. "Cocaine, Effects on the Developing Brain," *Annals of the New York Academy of Sciences*, 1998, Vol. 846.

Sızıntı Araştırma Grubu: "Terörde Psikofarmakolojik," *Sızıntı*, 2004, pp. 300, 595-597.

MARTYRDOM – A DEFINITION
Can a Terrorist Be a Martyr?

Hikmet Yüceoğlu

T o comprehend and solve a problem of any kind, the first thing that must be done is to identify the causes that have given rise to the problem. Otherwise, all analyses, comments, and methods of solution are destined to fail. If a glorious aim, like martyrdom, is the subject of wrongful acts, then there is an obvious need to evaluate this issue at length, and to base one's analysis on this assessment. However, our subject matter here will not focus on such an evaluation; rather it will be more of a search for the answers to what the place of martyrdom is, and who the martyrs in Islam are.

Ideal People

There are four types of people that are glorified as examples of ideal role models in the Qur'an and the Sunna, the two basic sources of Islam: the prophet, the *siddiq* (the eminently truthful person), the *shahid* (the martyr or witness) and the *salih* (the righteous person) (Nisa 4:69). The first one of these is the supreme culmination of the advancement and perfection that humanity can reach. But, this goal cannot be reached through effort or inspiration, for it is God Himself Who chooses the person to be sent as a prophet, and Who equips him with the necessary virtues. The way to this achievement was permanently closed after the last prophet, Muhammad, peace and blessings be upon him; there will be no other prophets. The other three statuses are truthfulness of heart, martyrdom, and righteousness.

The main factor in being a martyr is witnessing the truth in all aspects of life and in all of one's behavior. Even more so, martyrdom entails witnessing the truths of the ghayb, the unseen world, through an internal perception, in a way that is similar to how normal human beings perceive the physical world; this is the sense the Qur'an uses the words shahid and shahada (martyr-dom). Thus, to call those who have given up their lives for the sake of God martyrs or witnesses is a metaphor. They are called "witnesses" (martyrs) because they bear witness to the truth that they believe in so profoundly that they are willing to risk their lives for it.

Throughout history, martyrdom has always been one of the sublime degrees that Muslims aspire to achieve. At some point, martyrdom became the most important source of power in lead-ing Muslims to victory against enemies who were physically much stronger or of a greater number. Yet at other times, when Muslim soldiers had doubts about attaining martyrdom, defeat was the end result. For instance, the fact that Timur's army was also Muslim caused the Ottoman army to lose the Ankara War as Ottoman soldiers thought martyrdom and becoming a war hero (ghazi) would not be achieved in this war (Gökbilgin 1977).

Martyrdom is not only achieved by being killed by a non-Muslim soldier during a war; also such an event does not guaran-tee martyrdom. The death at the hand of a non-Muslim can occur due to many reasons that are not part of war. Even those who die because of brutality at the hand of a believer, or those who die by drowning, or poisoning, or from other similar causes, can be-come martyrs too. Thus, martyrdom is a spiritual rank, for which the willed intention of the individual is considered to be the es-sence of the issue. If this was not so, believers would ask to be killed by non-Muslims instead of desiring the martyrdom of God. In Islam, desiring to die is forbidden; believers must struggle to survive and win a war, rather than choosing to die. They become martyrs only when they fall dead after struggling to their utmost to survive the war. Thus, even if a person's intention is martyrdom, if they choose to die rather than struggle for the cause of God, then this could be considered as suicide—something which is forbidden in Islam. As a matter of fact, the Prophet and many of his Companions took precautions against death; they did not seek it out. They donned armor, and used shields during battles, they also retreated and dug trenches as necessary; in other words, they strove to survive and to win the war. Dying in a war is not the goal of a Muslim; and plunging into a war to meet this end could lead to a failure to attain martyrdom.

What Kinds of People Are Considered To Be Martyrs?

Martyrs are those who have followed the way that God has set out for believers, a way that leads to the blessings of God, and who have died or been killed while striving to fulfill the requirements of this way, or those who have died while protecting the values that God ordered to be protected; these people are praised and called martyrs.

Islamic literature generally mentions three classifications of martyrs: the perfect martyr, the martyr of this world, and the martyr of the afterlife.

The perfect martyr

Perfect martyrdom is the type that fulfills both the conditions of martyrdom in the sight of God and in which the burial rites suitable for a martyr are followed. During the burial of the perfect martyr 1) the ritual ablution of the body is not performed, 2) the body is not wound in a shroud, 3) and the funeral prayer is not observed—this last one is disputed.

There are six conditions for a martyr to be classified as a "perfect martyr":

1) To be a Muslim: the basic requirement is that the martyr be a believer (a Muslim.) It is determined that non-

Muslims cannot be beneficiaries of the spiritual blessings provided by Islam; these include the rank of martyrdom.

2) To be responsible: According to Islamic principles, for a person to be held responsible in Islam, he or she has to be of sound mental health and to have reached puberty. Therefore, children and mentally ill persons are not held to be responsible, thus making them illegible for "perfect martyrdom." This is the view of Imam A'zam; but scholars who oppose this view maintain that "those who reach puberty and those who do not are on equal footing regarding the conditions of martyrdom. Since those who have not yet reached puberty are considered to be Muslims, and if they die while fighting the infidels, then they have acted like those who have reached puberty. Thus, justice requires that they be treated equally. In fact, the treatment of the Prophet of the martyrs of 'the Battle of Uhud supports this view, because there were very young persons among the martyrs, like Harith ibn Numan" (Zuhayli 3:105).

3) Cleanliness: The martyr must be clean with regard to the conditions named as canonical impurity. According to this condition, men who are in need of ablution, and women who are in their menstrual period, or within the post partum period are excluded from the scope of the burial treatment of "perfect martyrs." That is to say that, those who are killed in this condition will be given ablution. This view, again, is according to Imam A'zam. On the other hand, other scholars, namely Imam Muhammad, Abu Yusuf, Shafii, Ahmet ibn Hanbal and Imam Malik argue that martyrdom itself cleans the impurity, thus there is no need for ablution to be given to persons killed in these conditions. The latter scholars substantiate their view with the case of Hanzala, who fought in the Battle of Uhud and was killed. He had been married the day before, and had run to fight without even having a

chance to make his ablution (which is required after intercourse). Even though his wife informed the Prophet that he was canonically impure when he died, the Prophet declared that he had been given ablution by the angels, and buried him without ablution (like all the other martyrs) (Ibn Abidin 3:514).

4) Not to be killed for a just cause: Those who are not killed for a just cause, for example as a legal punishment to a crime, such as *qisas* (retaliation killing), are considered to be "perfect martyrs."

5) Not to be a *murtas* (wounded person carried away from the battle field): This word, which literally means "a person wounded in a war, and carried to another location," includes those who undergo medical treatment, who eat, drink, sleep, have prolonged conversations, who make their last will, and things of this nature before dying. If all of these, which are regarded as worldly matters, happen after the person has been fatally injured and taken to another location, then the person is regarded as a *murtas*. If these actions are all engaged in at the place where one is injured, while the war is still being fought, then this does not alter the conditions of being a "perfect martyr." The case of 'Umar, 'Ali and 'Uthman (the second, fourth and the third caliphs) are perfect examples for this condition. 'Umar and 'Ali were transported to another place after being fatally injured, thus, their bodies were given ablution. However, 'Uthman, who died at the spot he was wounded, was not given ablution, and was subject to the procedures followed for a "perfect martyr."

6) Beyond the scope of blood money: In Islamic law, murder is punished by *qisas*, retaliation in kind. However, if the murder took place unintentionally or mistakenly *qisas* is not applied. For example, if the act is committed in a city, during the daytime, by an unforced kick, or by

hitting with any weapons and/or tools not made specifically for killing, like a whip (the usage of such a tool raises suspicion about the intention to kill) then retaliatory killing is not allowed. In short, according to Islamic Law, those who are the victims of a murder (in cases where the perpetrator is sentenced to retaliatory killing) are considered to be martyrs; whereas those who have been killed otherwise (that is, in a way that retaliation is not applied) are not considered to be martyrs (al-Kasani 1/321). Those who are killed while fighting against non-Muslims, outlaws, and rebels are considered to be martyrs, no matter how they die. Those who do not qualify for one of these conditions are not given the "perfect martyr" rituals in their funeral. (Yüce, 32-36)

A believer killed without a just cause is subject to the rules of "perfect martyr." On the battlefields, just as those who fall dead while fighting face to face with the enemy are martyrs; those who shoot themselves accidentally with their own weapons, or those who are shot by a comrade, or those who fall from their horse and are hit by the horse, or those who are trampled under the feet of the horses of either Muslims or non-Muslims, or those who are shot with a stray arrow, or anyone who is found dead for unknown reasons at the end of the war (even if there is no wound) are considered to be martyrs, and are treated with the burial rites of the martyr. The weapons and equipment of the past, such as horses, arrows, etc. that are given above can be replaced with today's equipments, for similar rulings.

Those who die in an enemy attack on a village, those who are killed by outlaws, those who are killed while providing secondary services, those who are killed in an attack on their home or working place, or those who are killed by their father intentionally are also martyrs. (Sarahsi 2, 52). If a group wages war against another group, even though they know that the other group is Muslim, then those who are killed on the defending side are martyrs. This is because those who are killed on the defending side have been killed while protecting themselves and the Muslim community (al-Ayni 3, 307). It can be concluded from this ruling that those who died on the attacking side are not considered to be martyrs, but rather are regarded as cruel sinners.

The martyr of this world

Those who fall dead in a fight with the enemy, and who are treated with the burial rites of a "perfect martyr," but who in fact are not martyrs and who will not be rewarded with the blessings of martyrdom, are called "martyrs of this world." These group includes those who died while deserting, or while looting,[1] or those whose real intention was not the will of God, but rather wanting to show off or to have revenge, or those who fought for other ideologies that contradict the principles of Islam, such as racism, or the gain of worldly goods (Zuhayli 2, 560). As it is very hard or even impossible to reveal these inner feelings, these people are treated like martyrs in this world. But their situation in the afterlife is depicted by the Prophet in the following words: "The first person to be judged unfavorably on the Judgment Day is the false martyr (the one known as such). He is brought up, and shown the rewards that would be given to him, which he recognizes. Then God asks him, "What did you do to get these rewards?" He answers "I fought for your sake until I fell martyred." Then God commands: "You are lying! You fought so that people could say 'What a brave man!' And so they did in the world, (you got what you asked for, you have already been paid)." Then it is commanded that this person be dragged to hellfire on his face."[2]

In another hadith, the following expressions are used (to describe the condition of "the martyrs of this world" in the afterlife): The Prophet was asked about what would happen to people who fought to gain possessions, or fame for their bravery, or who

---

[1] Muslim, *Iman*, 182.
[2] Muslim, *Imarat*, 152; Nasai, *Jihad*, 22.

fought for reasons of racism or bigotry, yet who were considered as having fought for the sake of God. He responded, "Those who fight to glorify the word of God are considered as fighting for the cause of God."[3] Here, this should be clarified; the essential intention is to gain God's consent and to glorify the religion of God; a person who works to this end can fight for other causes that serve the same goal. In that case, when he is killed, he is still a real martyr. However, this requires very sensitive commitment to the intention and feelings of the heart, and careful attention to the underlying goal.

One day, the Prophet asked, "Who do you call martyrs among yourselves?" The people around him answered, "Those who are killed with a weapon." His response to this answer was: "There are many who are killed with weapons, and they are not martyrs; there are many who die in their beds, but are rewarded with the blessings of the *siddiqs* (the eminently truthful ones), and of the martyrs." (al-Isfahani 8, 251). In another hadith, he drew attention to the damage caused by bad habits, stating that "Those who, every so often, shower the people around them with imprecations, will not be rewarded the *shafaa'* (intercession), nor they will be regarded as martyrs."[4] Today, there are people who claim to work for the cause of sacred values; yet they are not even satisfied with the imprecations they utter against those who think differently or who do not support them, and they go on to accuse these people of being infidels or pagans. However, the danger of such an approach is evident. In fact, when a believer is accused of being an infidel, it is the accuser who is, in fact, considered to be an infidel.[5] The Qur'an says:

> When you go to war in the cause of God, investigate carefully and do not say to anyone who offers you peace (salutation) "you are not of the believers." (Nisa 4:94)

---

[3] Bukhari, *Jihad*, 15; Muslim, *Imarat*, 149-151.
[4] Muslim, *Birr*, 85, 86; Abu Dawud, *Adab*, 45.
[5] Bukhari, *Adab*, 44.

While this verse does not approve of killing anybody who has indicated by their salutation that they are Muslim, murdering Muslims (along with non-Muslims) in suicide attacks and not paying heed to this issue needs to be discussed.

The martyr of the afterlife

These people are those who are killed in the way of a "perfect martyr," but who do not fulfill at least one of the six conditions listed above. They are not regarded as "martyrs of this world" but are classified as "martyrs of the afterlife." Those who were called martyrs by the Prophet and those who died, but were not killed, are also included in this category. The Prophet and Abu Bakr are regarded as such, because the poison they had imbibed at Haybar was effective. 'Umar and 'Ali are also considered as martyrs of the afterlife because they were transported from the place where they were wounded (thus not qualifying as perfect martyrs). It is recorded that the pinnacle of this category of martyrdom—with the exception of the Prophet—is that of 'Umar's.[6]

The martyr of the afterlife is given a regular funeral with its usual rites. That is to say, they are given ablution, wound in a shroud, and a funeral prayer is performed. This has not been a matter of dispute between scholars. However, in the afterlife, they will be given the rewards of the martyrs, and will be treated as such. The Prophet, on several occasions, has drawn attention to those who are considered martyrs among his the Muslim community. Even though there is no distinction in these hadiths, such as the "martyr of this world" and the "martyr of the after-life," the observations that the Prophet himself made have constituted the basis for the differentiations in the interpretations of scholars later periods.

Examining the hadiths concerning those who had been specified as martyrs but who were categorized as martyrs of the afterlife because they had not been given the burial rites of a

---

[6] Imam Malik, *Muwatta*, "Jihad," 36.

martyr, it can be seen that this group is comprised of the martyrs described above, and the ones that are legally regarded as martyrs. The latter describes death that occurs due to a serious illness, a death that cannot be avoided, or overcome, and a death that inflicts unbearable pain and suffering, or death due to accident, or while striving against tyranny, or when adhering to one's religion piously, or for being deprived of some of the goods of this world. God, who accepts every single hardship that a believer has to endure as compensation for sins, bestows the greatest rewards of martyrdom for those who undergo sufferings and pain that end in death. That is indeed, what can be hoped for from His Mercy. God Almighty, with his boundless mercy desires to forgive the sins of His Muslim servants and to exalt their degrees, so that they become eligible for Paradise and His presence; He has created ways to this end. He has informed us of these ways and methods through the words of the Prophet of Mercy, Muhammad, peace and blessings be upon him.

Suicide Attacks

Based on the general information provided above concerning martyrdom, we can now move on to focus on our subject matter, terrorism, suicide attacks and their relationship with martyrdom.

Based on the practices recorded in Islamic history,[7] the scholars of Islamic jurisprudence gave *fatwa*s (legal pronouncements) in the following line:

> It is permissible for a person to plunge into a group of enemy forces, or to attack them in cases where he hopes that he will be saved in the end, or—if there is no such hope—in cases where he will inflict damage on the enemy, and demoralize them, or will encourage his own combatants, or due to an extraordinary power he might feel, or in the case of a captive who is afraid that he will give up secret information. (Al-Shaibani 4/1512)

---

[7] See Bukhari, *Jihad*, 12; Muslim, *Imarat*, 145; Ibn Athir, 1/206; Ibn Hajar, 1/144.

A careful examination of this *fatwa* reveals that there are three major conditions required for martyrdom to be valid under such circumstances:

1) The situation in which the martyr finds themselves must be a state of war. The presence of two rival armies is required, where the combatant enemies have prepared for and come together to fight.

2) It is not absolutely certain that the attacker will die.

3) Death itself has been brought about by the other side.

The Claim of Effectiveness

Those who see suicide attacks as something permissible claim that there are no alternatives. They claim that the opposing side has incomparable advantages in terms of weapons, numbers, logistic support, facilities, military training, and that they are supported by the media. Thus, the claim is that there is no alternative to suicide attacks. This line of thinking brings with it two issues:

1) No distinction is being made here between the goal and the means employed to reach it; these two have been confused. For a believer, both the goal and the means that lead to the goal must be legitimate, and these two should not be confused. Since the ultimate goal is to achieve God's pleasure, the desire of achieving something at any cost should not replace this fundamental aim.

2) If any means at any cost was to be considered permissible if it led to the goal, this would then open the door to other illegal and inhumane activities, such as the employment of drug addiction or prostitution among rival groups to destroy their mental and moral health, the manipulation of science in order to produce harmful medicines instead of useful ones, the mistreatment of patients in hospitals, or the murder of them in one way or another in order to save resources. However, religion and the prophets that have

been sent to lead the people both to the happiness of this world and the afterlife have never used any inhumane methods nor have they approved of any such actions. Martyrdom is a rank achieved only when the principles of religion are observed; it cannot be reached by employing revenge and hatred. The methods that a Muslim employs must be as righteous as his or her purpose.

In addition to this fact, a Muslim cannot transgress the boundaries, even in wartime: *Fight in the cause of God those who fight against you, (but) do not transgress the limits; for God loves not transgressors* (Baqara 2:190). Sayyid Qutb briefly explains this verse as follows:

> Transgression can be seen as being aimed at women, children, the elderly and the members of the clergy of any religion who have devoted themselves to worship, or any other harmless and trustworthy people who are not participating in the war, and do not constitute a danger to either the effort of calling for Islam, or to the Muslim community. It (transgression) can also be understood as the violation of the rules of war as instituted by Islam. In fact, Islam has put forth the rules of war in question to minimize the cruelties of *jahiliyya* (ignorance) wars of both olden times and modern times, and to end these brutalities. These are the cruelties that Islamic sensitivity hates, and that Islamic piety is disgusted with.

After summarizing the practices of the Prophet and his companions, Sayyid Qutb ends his comments as follows:

> The Muslims knew that they had not won wars due to quantitative superiority, since their number was less. They also knew that the victory was not due to the superiority of their weaponry or equipment, since they had fewer weapons and equipment than their enemy. They achieved victory because of their faith, their devotion to God, and the help God gave to them. Thus, if

they had behaved in contradiction to what God and the Prophet had directed them, they would have deprived themselves of the only means to achieve victory. That is why they strictly observed the rules of war that were mentioned above, even against enemies who made them suffer unbearable agonies, and who killed some of their friends by unimaginable torture. (Qutb, commentaries on verse 2:290)

Types of Suicide Attacks

Examining suicide attacks that have been carried out around the world, we can see that they have occurred in two ways:

1) There are suicide attacks that are carried out systematically and resolutely by designated persons within the armies of two rival countries that are waging war against one another. Basically, this type of attack can be categorized into two sub-groups:

   a) The attack by a person or a group on a sizable enemy group or on a barracks with weapons, such as planes, tanks, hand grenades, etc. The examples drawn from Islamic history substantiate that such acts and the persons who carry out such attacks are considered to be martyrs if they die. But there is always a possibility that the attackers will survive these kinds of attacks.

   b) A person or a group of people tie bombs to their bodies, or load the vehicle that they are driving with bombs, and plunge into the midst of enemy soldiers, or into an enemy stronghold, exploding the bombs. This type of attack can only be permitted under very limited conditions that are put forth only by Islamic jurists, and can only be conceivable during an active war. Outside these circumstances, such attacks can only be destined as being incomprehensible, disgusting deeds, and they must be condemned. Some attacks are carried out in countries which are not even at war, countries which permit the attackers to enter the country, with a visa or without a visa, countries which permit the citizens of other countries to work, pursue an education, reside, open businesses, marry, and—if certain requirements are fulfilled—even to become a citizen. In this case the country on which the attack is carried out has taken both sides under its protection, allowing both sides to enter and reside there. The violation of this security means contravening and betraying the visa issued (in the words of Islamic law scholars, treachery against a sanctuary, refuge, and the right to free mobility); this is not permissible. Ibn Hajar Haythami considers the murder of a person with whom an agreement has been made as being one of the greatest sins (Az-Zawajir 2, 153).

2) These assaults, either directed toward foreigners, or the citizens or soldiers of another country with which the attacker may be at war, or by whom the attacker's country may be occupied, can be neither permissible nor comprehensible. The perpetrators cannot be called martyrs. Moreover, the person who perpetrates such a crime is also guilty of: a) killing innocent people, b) betraying and harming the state which granted visa, c) traumatizing people and creating psychological injuries, d) inflicting damage on the property of innocent people, e) if the perpetrator is a Muslim, then tarnishing the image of Islam, f) humiliating the country of which they are a citizen of internationally, g) making their families suffer, h) probably aiding the success of an international crime organization, i) if the attacker is Muslim, then making the enemies of Islam happy.... and finally, j) being responsible for an unforgivable crime. The grave responsibility of committing suicide and taking innocent lives (Muslim or non-Muslim) from the standpoint of religion is beyond the scope of this subject.

Conclusion

It is obvious from the framework of the abovementioned principles that there is no place for suicide attacks in Islam, and that the conditions, which give rise to these attacks, should be eliminated.

References

Gökbilgin, M. Tayyip. *Osmanlı Müesseseleri, Teşkilatı ve Medeniyeti Tarihine Genel Bakış*, Istanbul: 1977

Az-Zuhayli, Vehbi. *İslam Fıkhı Ansiklopedisi*. Ibn Abidin, *Redd al-Muhtar*; Shatibi, Mawkufat; Al-Kasani, *Badayi as-Sanayi*; Al-Ayni, *Al-Binaya*;

Yüce, A. *Şehitlik ve Şehitlerin Hayatı*, Istanbul: 2001

Sarahsi, *Al-Mabsut*; Mansur Ali Nasıf, *Gayat al-Ma'mul Sharhu at-Taj al-Jaim al-Usul*.

Qutb, Sayyid, *Fi zilal al Qur'an* [In the Shade of Qur'an];

Naim A. *Miras K. Tecrid Tercümesi*

Al-Isfahani, *Hilya al-Awliya*; Ibn Athir, *Usd al-Gabe*; Ibn Hajar, *Al-Isaba*, I, 144.

Ash-Shaibani, Muhammad. *Seerah al-Kabir*, (with commentaries); Al-Jassas, *Ahkam al-Qur'an*.

SUICIDE ATTACKS AND ISLAM

Ergün Çapan

Before starting to analyze suicide attacks, there are two general issues that need to be focused on. According to Islam, humans are superior because they are human. The Qur'an expresses this principle as *we have honored the children of Adam* (Al-Isra 17:70). Thus, regardless of a human being male or female, old or young, black or white, all human beings are venerable, inviolable, and protected. Islam regards human life very highly. Many verses of the Qur'an and the hadiths order that the five principle values,[1] known as the *"Zaruriyat al-Khamsa"* (the five indispensable conditions), must be protected. These conditions are; life, religion, progeny, the mind, and property. Thus, human life is not to be violated, honor is not to be desecrated, property is not to be confiscated. People cannot be driven away from their home or lands, they cannot be deprived of their freedom, and their right to practice their religion cannot be precluded. As Islam regards each human being as possessing the worth of the entire species, killing one person is deemed as being the equivalent of slaughtering the whole of humanity, and conversely, saving the life of one human being is considered the same as saving the life of humanity as a whole (Ma'ida 5:32).

Human beings are not as highly regarded on any commission or in any establishment for human rights or in any other religious

---

[1] Shatibi, *Muwafaqat*, 2/7-10

or belief system as they are in Islam. It is not permissible (in Islam) for a person to commit a crime even against him or herself; thus, taking the life that God bestowed upon one is forbidden. As, in the same vein, no person can take the life of another, nobody can end his or her life, i.e., suicide is not permitted. Islam categorically forbids suicide. The Holy Qur'an prohibits suicide (Nisa 4:29), and in many hadiths the Prophet declared that suicide is unlawful in Islam.[2]

Peace Is Essential in Islam

Islam means peace, security, and soundness. The Muslim who believes and practices this religion is a person who inspires trust in everybody, and even in everything; such a person does not harm anybody by word or by deed. In fact, Islam wages war against tumult, turmoil, discord, tyranny, and terrorism. As stated in several verses[3] of the Qur'an and in many hadiths,[4] peace is essential in Islam, and war is deemed as *arizi*, secondary, unnatural, or situational. The conduct of Muslims with other people should be based on the principle of peace as well. In fact, in a religion where security and world peace is the principle, war and discord are sure to be secondary; this is identical to the struggle of a healthy body that fights against the germs that have attacked it. Islam, in principle, does not tolerate war, even when there are strict regulations of how to carry it out, even though it is a reality of humanity and one of the most outstanding facts of human history. In Islam, war is restricted to the purpose of defense; within the framework of the principle mentioned in the Qur'an as follows, *tumult and oppression are worse than slaughter* (Baqara 2:191), war is justified only to prevent chaos (which leads to wars), anarchy, tyranny, and defeatism.[5] With the Qur'an, war

---

[2] Bukhari, *Janaiz*, 84; Muslim, *Iman*, 175.

[3] Muhammad 47:4; Al-Baqara 2:208; An-Nisa 4:90, 94; Al-Mumtahana 60:8. See Yazır, 1979, 4/2424. Zuhayli, *Asar al-Harb*, p.133-136.

[4] Bukhari, *Jihad*, 112, Muslim, *Jihad*, 19; Abu Dawud, *Jihad*, 89.

[5] Sarahsi, *al-Mabsut*, 10/5; Zuhayli, *Asar al-Harb*, 90-94

has been given a set of restrictions and principles for the first time in human history. (Gülen 2004, 238; Yazır 1979, 2/692)

Islam has put forth regulations to balance war. Islam considers justice and worldwide peace to be a principle, stating:

> O those who believe! Stand out firmly for God as witnesses to fair dealing and let not the hatred of others to you make you swerve to wrong and depart from justice. Be just: that is next to Piety: and fear God for God is well acquainted with all that you do. (Ma'ida 5:8)

Along with these fundamental principles, Islam acknowledges that every believer has the right to protect their religion, life, property, progeny, and their honor and sacred values. This is true to the extent that dying in defense of these rights is considered martyrdom. For instance, the Messenger of God stated that whoever is killed for the sake of their property is a martyr; whoever is killed defending their life is a martyr; whoever is killed protecting their relatives is a martyr; and whoever is killed for the sake of their home and family is a martyr.[6]

Having looked at the issue from this general perspective, we would like now to concentrate on suicide attacks. Suicide attacks should be analyzed in two groups; those committed in times of peace, and those committed during war.

Suicide Attacks in Times of Peace

First of all, it should be stated here that it would not be correct to take the laws and regulations that are pertinent to the state of war—a state that Islam regards as an *arizi* state of affairs—and apply them to times of peace. Laws of war apply only to times of war and warfare conditions. In times of peace and in civilian life Islam demands a high level of moral and religious values for each Muslim and demands that all people be treated with mercy

---

[6] Tirmidhi, *Diyat*, 21; Bukhari, *Mazalim*, 33; Muslim, *Iman*, 222.

and compassion; Islam strives to establish peace and security in society.[7] Thus, it is not possible that Islam would justify suicide attacks carried out in times of peace in any country against any target, civilian or military, as such attacks would result in the loss of innocent lives.

The Qur'an, which orders that all people and even all creatures be treated with mercy and compassion, equates *the slaying of a person unjustly* with *the slaying of the whole of humanity* (Ma'ida 5:32). Indeed, as mentioned above, from the Islamic point of view, killing a human being unjustly is as grave a crime as slaying the whole of humanity. This is because the unjust killing of a person implies both the possibility that any person can be killed indiscriminately, and advocates disrespect for the right to live for the whole of humanity. The person who commits such a crime embarks on a very terrible way with the murder of a human being, a creature that is very valuable to God. Thus, this perpetrator who savagely kills another human being deserves God's wrath and anger and should be punished in the Hereafter as if they had killed the whole humanity.

The Qur'an does not demand as harsh a punishment for any other crime as that which it passes on those who intentionally kill innocent human beings. The statement and the punishments are indeed terrifying:

> If a man kills a believer intentionally, his recompense is Hell to abide therein (forever): and the wrath and the curse of God are upon him and a dreadful penalty is prepared for him. (Nisa 4:93)

The punishment for the intentional murder of a believer is eternal hellfire, saving God's forgiveness. Ibn Abbas and some other scholars interpreted this verse as the repentance of those who killed a believer purposefully will be denied, and they will

---

[7] See Mumtahana 60:8; Jathiya 45:14

be doomed to eternal hellfire.[8] This commentary, made by the most prominent of authorities in the field of *tafsir* (commentaries on the Qur'an) deserves to be carefully considered.

It is stated in the verse, that in addition to the punishment of hellfire for those who intentionally kill a believer, these people are also condemned to God's wrath and damnation. A fearful torment is prepared for them as well. It is very important to make it clear here that there is no other threat as harsh or terrifying in the whole of the Qur'an. Likewise, the killing of an innocent human being is mentioned alongside committing *shirk* (speculating a partner to God, the particular major sin that will not be forgiven) (Furqan 25:68; An'am 6:151); the placing of these two together is also noteworthy in terms of illustrating the graveness of the matter.

Using Islamic sources to approve actions that take human life is not possible. No conscious Muslim who possesses the attributes of faith and Islam (submission to God) can commit such an act.

Suicide Attacks in a State of War

We have briefly outlined the general attitude of Islam to suicide attacks in times of peace. Now, we would like to analyze suicide attacks on civilians and innocent people in places where Muslims are in a position to fight for their lives, their sacred values, and their homeland from the perspective of Islamic criteria.

"Non-combatants" cannot be killed in the event of war

Every Muslim has to live his or her life in accordance with the principles of the message that God Almighty has revealed in the Qur'an. Muslims are supposed to structure each unit of their lives, from the realm of worship to social conduct and emotions, in compliance with divine guidelines. Thus, they are obliged to adhere to these guidelines while fighting for the defense of the

---

[8] Tabari, *Jami' al-Bayan*, 4/295; Ibn al-Kathir, *Tafsir al-Qur'an al-'Azim*, 2/332.

rights that must be protected. The process of war does not justify the violation of these principles and doctrines. Islam, even in the event of war, does not approve of the killing of non-combatant people who are elderly, women, or children; such people cannot possess the status of "combatant." And this approach, which is now considered as part of "the rules of engagement," is actually an original principle bequeathed to the law of war by Islam.

As a general principle, in the event of war "non-combatants" are not to be killed, as stated in the Qur'an:

> Fight in the cause of God those who fight you (who are liable and able to fight, and who participate actively in the fight) but do not transgress the limits; for God loves not transgressors. (Baqara 2:190)

The reservation of "those who fight you" in the original text of the verse is of extreme importance. To explain this in grammatical terms, the mood in Arabic denotes "participation" which, in this sense, means: "those who fall under the status of combatant." Thus, non-combatants are not to be fought against.

The "prohibition of the killing of non-combatants," as understood from this verse, was elucidated by the Prophet both verbally and by action: there are numerous hadiths on this subject.[9] However, we would like to narrate just a few of them here to clarify the issue:

In one of the expeditions (*ghazwa*), a corpse of a woman was found. The Messenger of God condemned this behavior stating, "But this woman was not a combatant, why was she killed?"[10] and then prohibited the killing of women and children.[11]

---

[9] See Tahawi, *Sharh al-Maan al-Asar*, 3/224-225; Tahanawi, *I'la as-Sunan*, 12/29.

[10] Abu Dawud, *Jihad*, 111.

[11] Bukhari, *Jihad*, 147; Muslim, *Jihad*, 25.

In addition, the Messenger of God used to warn the commanders and the armies he sent off to expeditions: "Fight in God's path, fight for God; abide by the agreement made between you and your rivals, if there is any; do not transgress limits; do not commit *musla* (the mutilation of a corpse, i.e., do not cut off the ears, noses, or the like, in other words, do not perpetrate the things that are humiliating to human dignity); do not kill children, women, the elderly, and those who take refuge in places of worship."[12]

After the Prophet, the Rightly Guided Caliphs (the first four Caliphs) followed these regulations with particular care, observing them meticulously. And from that day on, most Muslim heads of states reminded their commanders of these principles when they saw them off to the front, giving commands and inculcations which have been faithfully observed throughout history:

> Do not ever remove the fear for God from your heart. Do not ever forget that without God's *tawfiq* (divine guidance and assistance) you can do nothing. Always remember that Islam is the religion of love and peace. Courage, bravery, and the *taqwa* (fear of God, piety) of the Messenger of God must be your role model. Do not trample over sown fields and fruit gardens. Show respect to priests and monks who are living in places of worship, and to those others who have devoted themselves to God; do not harm them. Do not kill civilians, do not disrespect women, and do not treat the defeated ones in a humiliating manner. Do not accept gifts from the locals; do not lodge your soldiers in the houses of the locals. Never miss any of your five daily prayers. Fear God, and do not forget that death can come and find you at any time, even when you are thousands of miles away from the front line. Thus, always be prepared for death. (Gülen 2004, 238)

---

[12] Tahanawi, *I'la as-Sunan*, 12/31-32; Ahmad ibn Hanbal, *Musnad*, 1/300; Abu Dawud, *Jihad*, 82 Ahmad ibn Hanbal, *Musnad* 1/300; Baykhaki, *Sunan al-Kubra*, 9/90.

The scholars of Islamic law have unanimously agreed that the killing of non-combatant women, children, elderly people, monks, and the pious who are secluded in monasteries, engaged in worship, the blind and the handicapped is forbidden in Islam.[13]

In the aforementioned verse (Baqara 2:190) the Qur'an commands Muslims not to be excessive. "Being excessive" is defined in the comments of the Prophets in two ways: one, "killing non-combatants" and, two, "behaving degradingly towards those who are defeated." The Messenger of God prohibited the mutilation of the dead in war,[14] and also *sabran* killings (tying up a person while still alive to use as target practice and aiming at this person with a variety of weapons until the person is dead).[15] He even prohibited such practices being carried out on a chicken, let alone allowing it on humans.[16]

Additionally, God's Messenger drew attention to the fact that Muslims are obliged to behave in a fitting manner, even when fighting against the enemy: "Those who fight in a good manner (taking ethical and humane values into account) are the persons of belief."[17]

Islam even sets ethical rules and regulations on how to slaughter animals; therefore it is not to be wondered at that it prohibits excess when human beings fight one another. For centuries Muslims have been observing these ethical regulations when slaughtering animals in ritual sacrifices, as well as at other times. For instance, the ill treatment of animals and the sharpening of knives in front of their eyes are forbidden by a hadith.[18] In short, from the perspective of these criteria it can be clearly seen that the suicide attacks of today, which take hundreds of innocent lives, are in no way in accord with the general ethical principles of Islam.

---

[13] Tahawi, *Muhtasar al-Ikhtilaf al-Fuqaha*, 3/455-456.

[14] Bukhari, *Mazalim*, 30; Abu Dawud, *Jihad*, 110.

[15] Muslim, *Sayd*, 58-60; Ibn Maja, *Zabaih* 10. See Yazır, 2/694.

[16] Abu Dawud, *Jihad*, 120; Darimi, *Adahi*, 13.

[17] Abu Dawud, *Jihad*, 110; Ibn Maja, *Diyat*, 30.

[18] Abu Dawud, *Adahi*, 12; Tirmidhi, *Diyat*, 14.

Civilian targets cannot be attacked

Killing innocent people in war completely contradicts the fundamental principles of Islam. Neither during the time of the Prophet nor in the times of his Companions, or of the Tabiuns (the generation that followed the Companions) or in the periods that followed was such a method of war (i.e., the killing of innocent civilians) employed by Muslims; there is no precedent for these actions. As a counter-argument to claims like "there is no other choice," the fact that the Companions who were subjected to the harshest torture and ill treatment in Makka, and those who followed in later periods, never engaged in these kinds of actions is evidence enough.

In almost all sources of Islamic law there is discussion of one particular case: is it permissible for a Muslim during war to attack the enemy army or a unit of the same knowing that he is sure to be killed? The answer to this question is as follows: if he inflicts damage on the other side, and contributes positively to the struggle—i.e., if such an action were to boost morale and hearten the Muslims during war—then it is permissible for this person to do this action and to fight to the death. For instance, on the day of the Battle of Uhud, a group of the Companions did this (i.e., attacked the enemy in order to raise the spirit of Muslims) and they were praised by the Prophet. On the other hand, if such an attack would not inflict any damage on the military forces of the rival side, then such an action is not permissible. If the person were to continue in the attack knowing that it is of no benefit to the Muslims, then this person becomes the subject of the verse *God and cast not yourselves to perdition with your own hands, and do good (to others); surely God loves the doers of good* (Baqara 2:195).[19] It is not possible to take this case (of one person attacking an army) that is discussed in *fiqh* compilations as a basis for the justification of suicide attacks committed by tying bombs to one's body that are carried out on innocent crowds of

---

[19] Sarahsi, *Mabsut*, 10/37; Jassas, *Ahkam al-Qur'an*, 1/327; Ibn al Abidin, 1984, 4/127)

people. In the first place, the discussions in the *fiqh* books are concerned with times of war, and are discussing military targets, whereas suicide attacks are committed against civilian targets, against innocent people; thus, the two are completely separate subjects.

Another so-called proof that is put forth for suicide attacks is the issue of *tatarrus* that is mentioned in *fiqh* collections. It is permitted in the event of *tatarrus*, i.e., when the enemy uses Muslim prisoners of wars, women, and children, as human shields, for Muslims to attack the enemy while still taking as many precautionary measures as they can to protect the captives.[20] Again, this is also an issue pertinent to warfare, thus it cannot be used as a justification for suicide attacks against civilians and the innocent, i.e., non-combatants.

The word *irhab* as mentioned in the Qur'an

As known to Muslims, the words of praise mentioned in the Qur'an have a distinguished place. In particular, words mentioned only in the context of praise and honor have a very special significance. The word *irhab,* is an example to such words. The verse in which this word is mentioned in the Qur'an is as follows:

> Against them make ready your strength to the utmost of your power, including steeds of war to strike fear into (the hearts of) the enemies of God, and your enemies and others besides, whom you may not know, but whom God does know. Whatever you shall spend for the sake of God shall be repaid unto you and you shall not be treated unjustly. (Anfal 8:60)

---

[20] Sarahsi, *Mabsut*, 10/154; Tahawi, *Muhtasaru Ikhtilaf al-Fuqaha*, 3/43.

Therefore, those who believe in the Qur'an and hold it as their reference must approach this word with the respect and dignity which it deserves.

The literal meaning of the word *irhab* mentioned in the verse is "to frighten." However, this is a natural "fright" which arises against the possibility of harm and which acts as a deterring force; it is not harming oneself.[21]

*Mufassir*s (the Islamic scholars who are proficient commentators on the Qur'an) have interpreted the word *irhab* mentioned in the verse as meaning to be equipped with the necessary weapons (such as steeds of war) against the enemy in order to create a deterring force in accordance with the conditions of the day.[22]

Rashid Ridha states that the word *irhab* means not to wage a war, but on the contrary, to prevent war; thus, implying the protection of society, not the destruction of it. He also interprets the aforementioned verse as "preparing the weapons of war to the greatest degree possible, in order to prevent the enemies—known or not—from waging a war or attacks."[23]

In hadiths, the word *irhab* denotes deterrence,[24] and in the commentaries of the hadiths it is interpreted as such.[25] An-Nihaya, which compiles uncommon words (*garib*) in the hadiths, explains the word *irhab* as one's being so powerful that one is able to deter the enemy from attacking and to deter the enemy altogether.[26]

The Companions interpreted this verse as being prepared for warfare, and having a deterrent power. For example, during the reign of 'Umar, there were forty thousand thoroughbred Arabian horses maintained at the ready on one of the farms near Madina;

---

[21] See Ibn al Manzur, *Lisan al-'Arab*, "r-h-b"; Raghib, *Mufradat*, "r-h-b"; Zabidi, *Taj al-Arus*, "r-h-b."

[22] Tabari, *Jami al-Bayan*, 6/42; Razi, *Mafatih*, 15/192; Alusi, 10/26; Yazır, *Hak Dini Kur'an Dili*.

[23] Rashid Ridha, *Tafsir al-Manar*, 10/66.

[24] Bazzar, *Musnad*, 6/30; Ahmad ibn Hanbal, *Musnad*, 3/493.

[25] Azim Abadi, *Awn al-Ma'bud*, 8/159

[26] Ibn Athir, *an-Nihaya fi Gharib al-Hadis*, 2/262

these horses did not go to war, even though there had been confrontations on several fronts. Likewise, near Syria, forty thousand more horses were kept at the ready on reserve. These horses, which were among the most important weapons of war in that time, were being maintained as reserve forces just in case.[27]

As another meaning of the word *ribat* denotes devoting, dedicating, or assigning some members, either human or animal, to some places, it is possible to interpret the word *ribat* mentioned in the verse as being prepared and prudent in such ways. Thus, the Qur'an sets a goal for us as if it were ordering us "to defend and protect our religion, honor, reputation, dignity, our homeland, and all sacred values against the enemies who have malicious intentions; to take all the measures necessary to maintain such power that enables us to do so; and not to give any chance to the enemy."[28]

The scholars of Islamic law also used the word *irhab* to mean being a deterrent.[29]

As a result, when we examine the structure of the word *irhab*, its usage, and the meaning that has been given to it in hadith books and commentaries, in the books of Islamic law, and in dictionaries, the following facts come to light:

1) The word *irhab* as mentioned in the Qur'an is related to the issue of *i'dad*; this is a word that means being ready to defend one's sacred values. It aims at preventing transgressions, at precluding tyranny, and at reprimanding the perpetrators of crimes. This issue has been recognized and accepted among societies and nations since the beginning of history, and does not contradict humane values. Who

---

[27] Mawlana Shibli an-Numani, *Bütün Yönleriyle Hazreti Ömer ve Devlet İdaresi*, Istanbul: Hikmet Yayınları, 1986. Translated by Talip Yaşar Alp.

[28] See Gülen, *Sonsuz Nur*, 2/190-192

[29] See Sarahsi, *Mabsut*, 10/42; Ibn al-Qudama, *al-Kafi*, 40264; Bahuti, *Kashshaf al-Ghina*, 3/65; Abu Ishak, ash-Shirazi, *Muhazzab*, 2/231; Ibn al-Abidin, 6/305.

can deny the need for deterrents to daunt criminals, tyrants, aggressors, and invading enemies?

2) Muslim scholars use the word *irhab* in their works to mean
"to discourage the enemy before or during the war, to
daunt, and to demoralize spiritually and psychologically."

In the past, these deterrents took on different forms, such as
dressing oneself in silk, dying gray hair black, putting on orna-
ments and jewelry, decorating the sword and its sheath with gold
embroidery and designs, confronting an army by oneself, and
preparing and training many horses for war. All of these were in
accordance with the realities of the conditions of warfare at that
time.[30]

Other than the two forms mentioned above, there is no other
usage of the word *irhab* in either the Qur'an or in the Sunna, nor
can it be found in other written works that originate from the
Qur'an or the Sunna. Thus, it would not be correct to interpret
the word *irhab* that is mentioned in the Qur'an to mean killing
innocent people in public areas by tying bombs to one's body,
the shedding of blood, the setting of fires, causing damage to
houses or property, spreading horror in order to introduce chaos
into society nor the use of the Qur'an as proof supporting these
actions.

Additionally, there is another significant issue that must be
focused on: all of the classical Arabic dictionaries provide only
the word *ihafa* (to frighten) as the definition of the word *irhab*.
Nevertheless, it has been noticed that in some dictionaries com-
piled in the second half of the twentieth century the definition of
the word *irhab* has been changed and modified. Intentionally or
not, in particular in dictionaries prepared by non-Muslims, the

---

[30] Muhyiddin al-Ghazi, "Adwaun ala Kalimat al-irhab," *al-Bas al-Islami*, No. 48, p. 84;
See Ibn al-Abidin, 6/756.

word *irhab* has been defined as "terrorism."[31] However, it is quite clear that there is an obvious difference between the word *irhab*, which means "frightening with a deterring power before engaging in a war" and the word "terrorism" which denotes killing, bombing, arson, spreading horror, and committing acts of violence that drive society into chaos.[32]

A judicial decision cannot be passed on an unspecified issue

One of the primary practices of the methodology of Islamic law is that the determination of the boundaries of the subject matter precedes the final establishment of the judgment. Thus, it is not possible to make decisions on unspecified issues that have no specified frame or boundaries, as to do so would open the way to misconduct and abuse.

If suicide attacks are considered from this perspective, it becomes obvious that the target is not determined and who will be killed is not known. These attacks are carried out everywhere, in all places that are open to public life, such as street-markets, shopping areas, restaurants, bus stations, etc., where people pursue their daily activities; women, children, the elderly, Muslims, non-Muslims, all of these are targeted without discrimination. Thus, attempts to carry out such attacks, attacks where the goal and the target group are not determined, are in sheer opposition to one of the general principles of Islamic law.

In Islam the principle is the individuality of the crime

In Islam the penalties are peculiar to the case: whoever commits a crime is the only person to be called to account, and it is this

---

[31] *Oxford Wordpower*, New York: Oxford University Press, 1999; Hans Wehr, *A Dictionary of Modern Written Arabic*, Beirut: Maktabat al-Lebanon, 1960; *English Arabic Glossary*. See *Encyclopaedia Britannica*, 11/650-651.

[32] See Muhyiddin al-Ghazi, *al-Bas al-Islami*, No. 48, pp. 85-86; Dr. Jallul ad-Dakdak, "Hirabuyyun la irhabiyyun," *al-Mahajja*, No. 208, pp. 5-6, February 15, 2004.

person alone who serves the sentence. As repeatedly stated in the Qur'an, *no bearer of burdens can bear the burden of another* (An'am 6:164; Nahl 17:15; Fatir 35:18). The individuality of the crime and the penalty imposed is a principle of Islamic law. The targets of suicide attacks are innocent civilians; the fact that these attacks are aimed at innocent people is not in accord with this fundamental principle of law. Therefore, these attacks can only be considered to be unjust and contradictory to the Islamic understanding of justice.

Suicide attacks defame the essential identity of Islam that is based on love and tolerance

The means employed to reach a certain end must be as legitimate as the end itself. As mentioned earlier, a person's struggle to protect their sacred values, property, or nation are among the essential duties of humanity. Risking one's life for the sake of these sacred goals is the way to martyrdom. Conversely, adopting an unjustifiable means to reach such a goal results in divine reproach, and will yield exactly the opposite outcome; making things difficult for all Muslims. However, the Messenger of God, peace and blessings be upon him, his Companions, and the Muslims who have followed them as representatives of peace and serenity have always protected the identity of Islam during times of peace and war alike, and have never let it fall into disrepute. Today, Muslims are thought to be equated with "terrorism," and thus it has become obligatory for them to distance themselves as much as possible from any behavior or action that could be used to make such an incorrect and unfair accusation.[33] It is only because a few Muslims in a few places have behaved in this way or have endorsed those who carry out such actions that the words "Islam" and "terror" have been used conjointly, tarnishing the

---

[33] Cevdet, Said. *Islami Mücadelede Şiddet Sorunu* [The Problem of Violence in Islamic Struggle], pp. 65-67.

image of Islam; the way for those who want to bring disgrace onto Islam has been cleared.

When Muslims in different parts of the world, frustrated by the hardship to which they are subjected, choose suicide attacks as their only way to fight, this decision does not only affect them; it is of concern to all Muslims. As a matter of fact, any suicide act involving the use of bombs in any place anywhere in the world brings infamy to the name of Islam and to all Muslims.

We would like to narrate an incident that took place in this century concerning this matter: Bediüzzaman Said Nursi enrolled as a volunteer commander in a regiment during World War I, and served his people and country in' a devoted manner. During the war, Armenian guerrillas slaughtered women and children in some places, and in retaliation, in some places, Armenian children were killed. Thousands of Armenian children gathered in the township where Said Nursi governed. He ordered the soldiers that "no harm will be done to them," later setting free these Armenian children and returning them to their families on the Russian side of the border. This kind of behavior by Nursi constituted an exemplary lesson for the Armenians, and earned their admiration for Muslim moral values. They promised not to kill Muslim children, saying that "since Molla Said did not slaughter our children and returned them to us, from now on we will not kill Muslim children." Because of Nursi's behavior and his approach, which were in accordance with the spirit of Islam, many Muslim children were saved from being slaughtered. [34]

Conclusion

Muslims must adhere to the criteria of their religion both in times of peace and in times of war. They have to control their feelings in accordance with the essential principles of Islam, no matter how difficult are the conditions or the severity of the suffering

---

[34] Nursi, Bediüzzaman Said. *Tarihçe-i Hayatı*—İlk Hayatı [Bediüzzaman's Biography—First Phase] Risale-i Nur Collection, p.2134.

that has to be endured. They must not engage in any kind of action which Islam does not approve of. It is a great crime to commit suicide attacks during times of peace. There is absolutely no way that Islam would approve of such cold-blooded murders. And it is not possible that any conscious Muslim who has faith would commit such an act.

Suicide attacks on civilian targets during times of war are not permissible, because these attacks target women, children, the elderly, and other non-combatant civilians, whom Islam prohibits the killing of in times of war. Moreover, murdering innocent, harmless people causes terror and anarchy, tarnishing the image of Islam and harming all Muslims.

Even though Muslims in all sectors and classes suffer hard times in some countries, suicide attacks can never be justified. Carrying out attacks on undetermined targets and unspecified people, tying bombs to one's own body for the sole purpose of killing and detonating these explosives in a crowd of innocent people and children cannot be considered Islamic behavior. Islam has set rules and principles on "how to kill and be killed and how to fight with the enemy" during wartime; these are not to be violated, no matter the ferocity of the battle. In Islam, there is no such thing as killing women, children or other innocent people who are not actively participating in the war. In conclusion, while sharing the misery caused by the helplessness of our Muslim brothers and sisters, we would like to express that this method of fighting which Muslims have been drawn into is wrong, and that Islam and all believers have been condemned because of the erroneous manner of a minority who has chosen this inhumane way as a method of struggle.

References

Azim Abadi. *Awn al-Ma'bud*, Beirut: Dar al-Kutub al-Ilmiyya, 1994.

Bazzar Abu Bakr. *Musnad al-Bazzar*, Beirut: Muassasat al-Ulum al-Qur'an, 1988.

Yazır, Elmalılı M. Hamdi. *Hak Dini Kur'an Dili*, Istanbul: Eser Yay., 1979.

Gülen, Fethullah. *Sonsuz Nur*, Nil Yay. Izmir, 2003.

──. *Toward a Global Civilization of Love and Tolerance*, New Jersey: The Light, Inc., 2004.

Hans Wehr. *A Dictionary of Modern Written Arabic*, Beirut: Maktabat al-Lubnan, 1960.

Ibn al-Abidin, Muhammed Emin. *Haşiyetü Reddi'l-Muhtar*, Istanbul: Kahraman Yay., 1984.

Al-Mahajja, No: 208, February 15, 2004.

Mevlana Şibli en-Numani. *Bütün Yönleriyle Hazreti Ömer ve Devlet İdaresi*. Translated by Talip Yaşar Alp. Istanbul: Hikmet Yayınları, 1986.

Muhyiddin al-Ghazi. "Adwaun 'ala Kalimat al-irha." *al-Bas al-Islami,* Lekne: Muassasat as-Sahafa wannashr, May, 2003.

Oxford Wordpower, Oxford University Press, New York, 1999

Seyyid Bey. *el-Medhal*, Istanbul.

Shatibi, Ibrahim ibn Musa. *al-Muwafaqat fi Usul ash-Sharia*, Beirut: Dar al-Kutub al-Ilmiyya.

Tahawi, Abu Jafar. *Muhtasar al-Ihtilaf al-Fuqaha* (Ihtisar, Jassas). Abdullah Nazir Ahmad, Dar al-Bashair al-Islamiyya, Beirut, 1996.

Sharh, *al-Maan al-Asar*, Beirut: Dar al-Kutub al-Ilmiyya, Lebanon, 1987.

Zuhayli, *Asar al-Harb fi'l-fıqh al-Islami diraseten ve mukareneten*, Syria: Dar al-Fikr, 1998.

VIEWS ON THE RULES OF WAR IN ISLAMIC LAW

Ahmet Güneş

Terror is a social phenomenon that unfortunately is still on the agenda. As is known, social phenomena cannot be explained with a single reason. The psychology of terrorism, its historical background, its political, economic, and sociological reasons, and the suggestions for solutions are subjects of the relevant disciplines. And it is a serious shortcoming on the part of the discipline of law that the content and the boundaries of the definition of the term "terrorism" have still not been specified. Nevertheless, it is only common sense to depict events that target the lives of innocent people as terrorism.

Another major problem is that terrorist events are being mentioned conjointly with the religion of Islam. The basis of this problem is grounded on incorrect and biased interpretations. Biased interpretations are the subject of another discussion; but the incorrect interpretations that have arisen due to variations in the understanding of the moods of the verbs to fight (*qital*) and to kill (*qatl*) that appear in the verses of the Qur'an will be dealt with here.

It is the basic principle in Islam that the right to life, honor, and property of a person are inalienable. Thus, any crime that violate the sanctity of the life, honor, and property of a person is punished by the sanctions of this world or of those in the hereafter. It is clearly stated in the Qur'an that murdering a person is the same as murdering all of humanity, and that enabling a person to live, correspondingly, is the same as giving life to all people. The importance of human life in Islam has been emphasized in all its different dimensions (Ma'ida 5:32). Moreover, the penalty for killing people who belong to a group which is a party with an agreement with the Muslims has been specifically determined in the Qur'an (Nisa 4:92). This has been extended to cover people who do not belong to the tribe bound by the agreement (Yazır, 2/1420-1421). According to Abu Hanifa, if a Muslim kills a non-Muslim, then the same penal procedure is applied (Kasani 1986, 7/252). Since the main priorities of the Islamic system is to protect public security, law and order, the security of property and lives, and freedom of mobility, then crimes violating the security of life and the property of people (*khiraba*) are regarded within the framework of the Islamic penal code of *Hadd* (crimes that are subject to capital punishment). The Qur'an orders that the perpetrators of such crimes should be sentenced to heavy sanctions in this world, while it is declared that their punishment in the hereafter will be even more dreadful (Ma'ida 5:33).

In Islamic law, wars are regarded differently. Even rebellions are considered to fall within the category of war. In the Qur'an, even though the words *harb* and *ghaza* exist, the word most frequently used to denote war is *qital*. The Qur'an tells of historical wars, wars between two Muslim groups, and more frequently, wars between Muslims and non-Muslims.

War in Islamic Law

Muslim scholars of law have engaged in collecting and ordering judicial decisions related to the state of war, starting from the earliest times of Islamic history. Compilations of certain kinds of books under the name of *seerah* date back to AH 2 (623). These books are the first examples of a unique type in the world literature which studies war in judicial terms. Imam Muhammad wrote *Kitab al-Seerah al-Saghir* which includes the views of Abu Hanifa on the subject. Awzai criticized some of the views recorded in this book. And Abu Yusuf went on to answer these criticisms in his work entitled *Ar-Raddu ala Seerah al-Awzai*. Later on, Imam Muhammad composed his more detailed work *Kitab al-Seerah al-Kabir* (Yaman 1998, 38). There have been many commentaries written on both of the books by Imam Muhammad, as these were the main references for the Hanafi school of thought. During the Ottoman era, the commentary by Sarahsi, *Kitab al-Seerah al-Kabir* was translated into Turkish and was included in curriculum for the military schools (Bursalı 1972, 1/407). The Islamic laws relating to the state of war and peace have been systematized into special sections, namely *seerah* in the *fiqh* (Islamic law) literature, which is based on the laws contained in the Qur'an and how our Prophet implemented these, i.e., hadiths. In these sections, the religious and judicial issues of pre-war and post-war are detailed. Important elements are discussed, for example, the contract of *Zimmat* between non-Muslims and the consequences, the institution of *eman*, international agreements, and even trade relations with non-Muslim states. The battles of Ridda, and the judicial decisions relating to the Khawarij Rebellion of Baghy are among the chapters that make up these books (Semerkandi 1984, 3/293).

In Islamic law, war is examined in terms of its basic tenets and separately in terms of its subdivisions. In the methodology of Islamic law, the term *hasen* (good) is examined as part of the discussion of the *hasen-kubh* (good-bad) issue in two categories: *hasen ilaynihi* (essentially good) and *hasen ligayrihî* (good owing to other factors/good because of the end result). In this classification, wars are considered to be *hasen ligayrihi*: in other words, wars are not essentially good, because they are the cause of things that are not good, such as the taking of lives and the destructions of countries; however, wars are considered to be good owing to their role in the protection of religion, the security of lives, property, and physical and mental health, and progeny (Kasani 1986, 7/100; Bilmen 3/380).

In the doctrine of Islamic law, there are various views concerning the issue of war as it relates to international relations. While from one perspective, all international relations with non-Muslim states seem to be based on war, there are others—especially according to the scholars of the Hanafi school—who consider anything to do with infidelity (*kufr*) to be among the "Rights of God" (issues between God and the person). Therefore the judgment of such situations is left to be judged in the Hereafter, as this is essentially a matter between God and the individual (Sarahsi 1997, 4/186). Essentially, international relations are based on peace. This principle is codified as *to you your religion and to me mine* (Kafirun 109:6), and *to us our deeds and to you yours* (Baqara 2:139; Qasas 28:55; Shura 42:15).

Even though there is no negative element in the fundamentals of Islamic belief, in its ethical code or in its social manifestations, the Qur'an poses questions in some places concerning accusations made against the Prophets; while at other times it inquires what the crimes of Muslims were. For instance, while the story of an anonymous man is narrated—a man who had chosen to keep his faith secret until a point came when he blurted it out—the verse reads *will you slay a man because he says 'my Lord is God'?*" (Ghafir 40:28). Abu Bakr once, used the same verse against the pagans (Ibn Hisham 1/290). From the same standpoint, the case of Muslims is described in the following verses:

> They have been expelled from their homes in defiance of right (for no cause) except that they say, "Our Lord is God." (Hajj 22:40)

> They have driven out the Prophet and yourselves (from your homes) (simply) because you believe in God your Lord. (Mumtahana 60:1).

In the verses pertinent to war, the actions of enemies are depicted in a variety of ways:

> They would not cease fighting the Muslims until they turn them back from their faith if they could. (Baqara 2:217)

> They fight you for your faith. (Mumtahana 60:8)

Interestingly, it is explained that the permission to fight is given *because they (Muslims) have been wronged (victimized)* (Hajj 22:39). The other statements of reasons consist of the following: the enemies are the first to assault (Tawba 9:13); that they (enemies) do not respect the covenants, that they break the agreements (Tawba 9:8, 10); and that they are treacherous (Anfal 8:58).

As Sarahsi has pointed out, the statements of reasons for going to war are either explicitly illustrated, or implicitly referred to (Sarahsi 1986, 10/110). The Qur'an tells of a great number of enemies *coming on you from above and from below you* (Ahzab 33:10). Our Prophet also employed such expressions as "all of the Arabs have made you the target of an alliance." In another instance, in the event of *ila*,[1] the expression "is it the Ghassanids who attacked?" was used by 'Umar. The fact that the leader of the Ghassanids considered Madina to be *dar-ı hawan* (a despicable place) even after Tabuk expedition illustrates the nature of such relations.[2] However, a healthier evaluation of this matter demands information on the positions of the Sassanids and the Byzantium against Madina (the Muslim State).

---

[1] *Ila*: (Literally, a form of divorce) The Prophet deserted his wives for a month after they asked to be subsided more as they were living under dire conditions. Then, the verses Al-Ahzab 33:28, 29 were revealed where his wives were given two options, whether to choose the present life and its finery, or God and His Messenger. As the Companion guarding the Prophet's house rushed to 'Umar in panic to inform about this extraordinary event of *ila*, 'Umar inquired whether Ghassinids attacked, as Muslims were always under the threat of a possible attack from other tribes.

[2] Bukhari, *Maghazi*, 79; Muslim, *Tawba*, 53.

The Prophet and Diplomatic Solutions

When the Prophet, peace and blessings be upon him, came to Madina, the first thing he did was to sign a treaty with the Jewish inhabitants of the city (Waqidi 1966, 184). History books recorded many agreements—relating to religion or politics—that the Prophet made with many tribes. The scholar Muhammad Hamidullah established that "the Messenger of God had already formed an alliance with a branch of the Juhayni Tribe in the first year of the Emigration, and historical records show that he signed alliance treaties with the Bani Demre, the Bani Mudlij, the Bani Zur'a and the Bani Rab'a within the second year" (Hamidullah 1987, 75). The same author, in his work *Majmu'a al-Wasaik al-Siyasiyya,* has records of agreements the Prophet made with hundreds of tribes. The Prophet, before signing the Hudaybiya Treaty, said that "Pity on that Quraysh! The war has ruined them. What if they had not become between me and the rest of the Arabs! If they win, that is what they want; but if God makes me dominate over them, they will submit to Islam altogether. Even if they are strong now, how long will they continue to fight?" (Abu Yusuf 1910, 208).

During the signing of the Hudaybiya Treaty, even though the dramatic case of Abu Jandal, who was tortured because he had converted to Islam, took place before everybody's eyes, and even though all of the Prophet's companions objected to this (i.e., leaving Abu Jandal being outside the protection of the Muslims), the Prophet signed the treaty (Waqidi 1966, 2/612). Subsequently, after signing this treaty, chapter Fath (Conquest) was revealed. And the Companions of the Prophet recorded that many people chose Islam as they now had an opportunity to meet one another as a result of this treaty. This happened to such an extent that the new converts to Islam after this treaty outnumbered the number of people who became Muslim before the treaty (Waqidi 1966, 2/607-610).

There were occasions when the Prophet was obliged to fight in wars. The reasons why these wars occurred are detailed in history books. According to historical accounts, the reason for a war was never solely a difference in belief, nor was it ever the sole reason for any expedition that the Prophet undertook (for details, see Waqidi, *Maghazi;* Hamidullah, *Battlefields of the Prophet Muhammad).*

As it is commonly known, there are two types of solutions for international conflicts; the first is a political solution, while the second is the deployment of power. The utilization of power is the last resort to be used, and this only in case all diplomatic solutions fail. The Prophet tried to find diplomatic solutions—to whatever extent possible—when relations became hostile. During the time he spent in Makka, the Muslims were under constant assault by the Quraysh pagans. To escape from torture some Muslims emigrated to Abyssinia (modern day Ethiopia), while the pagans attempted to sabotage this move. Because of this, the Prophet and most of his Companions were obliged to emigrate to Madina. With this background, the relations between the Muslims in Madina and the Quraysh in Makka can be considered as having become hostile due to the behavior of the Makkan pagans. It was because of this de facto situation that the Prophet sent out expedition groups to gather intelligence and to insure security.

The Prophet wanted to blockade the Makkan caravan under the leadership of Abu Sufyan who was returning from Syria, due to the fact that the caravan was, for the most part, made up of possessions plundered from the Muslims. However, Abu Sufyan, having been informed of this, took the caravan to Makka via an alternate route, following the coastline. Nevertheless, having received this information, the Quraysh made preparations for war, and set out. The two groups (the Muslims who were waiting for the return of the caravan, and the Quraysh) unexpectedly met at the conjunction of the Makka-Syrian caravan route and the Madina route. The Qur'an clearly states that the intention of the Muslims was only to attack the caravan (Anfal 8:7). The fact that the Prophet met with the leaders of the tribes to discuss the possibility of war also proves that the intention was not to wage a war. In the end, the Prophet sent 'Umar out to deliver a proposal of peace, but this was not enough to change the result (Waqidi 1966, 1/61).

It is internationally acknowledged that an attack on one party of an alliance is considered to be an attack on all the members of an alliance. The Arab tribes freely formed alliances with either the Muslims or with the pagans of Makka, as stipulated in the Hudaybiya Treaty. The Bani Bakr tribe became an ally of the Quraysh and the Huzaa Tribe, yet later formed an alliance with the Muslims. However, with the help of the Quraysh, some people from Bani Bakr killed some Muslims from the Huzaa Tribe in a nighttime attack. When this incidence was reported to the Prophet, he immediately investigated the matter. Once the involvement of the Quraysh had been established, the Prophet sent a Companion named Damra as an envoy to present various alternatives: either the head money for those who had been killed from Huzaa would be paid, or the alliance agreement with the tribe in question (i.e., Bani Bakr) would be revoked. If either of these conditions were not met this would mean that the Quraysh had annulled the Hudaybiya Treaty. The Quraysh did not accept either of these alternatives, and the envoy returned to Madina empty-handed. Subsequently, the Quraysh sent Abu Sufyan to renew the treaty, however, this attempt was also unsuccessful and the Treaty was annulled (Waqidi 1966, 2/783-844).

The Rules for War in Action

In the dictionary, the word *qital* (war) is derived from the root *qatl* (to kill). Thus, war requires killing and being killed. The Qur'an uses the word *qatl* to denote both killing and being killed, with regard to both Muslims and enemies alike (Tawba 9:111). Nevertheless, killing is not something a Muslim can be proud of. It is for this reason that it is a religious duty for a Muslim to adhere to certain rules and regulations that are used to establish whether or not there is an active war. These rules can be summarized as follows:

The first rule of an active war is the existence of a state of war. There are two types of wording in the verses that are related to wars: in some verses, as in the verse *if they fight you slay them* (Baqara 2:191), the permission to take life is restricted to being in a state of war.

Chapter Tawba has a special importance, for it was the last chapter to come that dealt with decisions related to war. In this chapter of the Qur'an, while it is stated that some of the agreements made with some of the tribes have ended, it is ordered that the agreements which had not been invalidated by other tribes should be abided by. It is important to note that in this context both groups of tribes (those who rebuked the agreements and those who adhered to them) are described as pagans (Tawba 9:1-4). Additionally, it is decreed in the verse that those pagans who ask for protection should be given the same (Tawba 9:6).

The second rule in Islamic law concerning war is that the enemy has to be a combatant. Those who are not combatants are regarded as innocent. Under this criterion of innocence, priests and monks cannot be assaulted, civilians cannot be harmed, children cannot be hurt, and women, even those who are serving the combatants behind the lines by cooking or nursing the wounded, cannot be killed, even if found in the field of war. When the Prophet saw a woman lying dead in the field of war, he protested: "But she was not a combatant" (Sarahsi 1997, 1/32). However, if these groups actively participate in the war as soldiers, then they are outside the scope of this general protection (Sarahsi 1986, 10/110).

The third rule of war in Islamic law is the existence of actual harm inflicted by the enemy. According to this rule, those combatants who do not inflict any harm on the Muslims cannot be killed, even in the field of war. As is known, those enemies who do not cause any harm in the field of war are taken as prisoners of war. The Qur'an offers the alternatives of setting the captives free in exchange for something or even with nothing in return (Muhammad 47:4). The Prophet always treated prisoners of war fairly, making sure that they were provided with food and water, and he usually preferred setting them free. It is narrated in the Qur'an that, despite their high level of destitution, the Muslims fed the captives, no matter what their belief, without expecting any worldly recompense, without even expecting any gratitude from them; rather they did all this only for the sake of God (Insan 76:8-9).

The Prophet never cursed his greatest enemies, even in a time of war. He prayed for those who were determined to kill him and all Muslims, saying, "O God, they are your servants as well; just like us, your servants" (Sarahsi 1997, 1/56).

It is not only humans that the Qur'an shows concern for. The Qur'an relates a story concerning a queen ant in the context of the story of the Prophet Solomon. The ants were instructed to enter their home by the queen as precaution against the possibility of being trampled unwittingly by Solomon and his army (Naml 27:18). It certainly is possible to consider all living creatures in the same category: not only animals, but also vegetation is included. It was clearly declared by the Prophet and by the first four caliphs of Islam in their instructions for warfare that the natural vegetation and fruit trees were not to be harmed (Waqidi 1966, 3/1117).

The Prophet, peace and blessings be upon him, prohibited the mutilation of the bodies of slain enemies, such as the cutting off of their ears or noses, or the removal of their eyes (*musla*).[3] He, as he valued humans merely for being human, also instructed the Muslims that they should not speak unfavorably about the deaths of the enemy, therefore preventing their relatives who were still alive from being insulted.[4]

Muhammad Hamidullah noted that—including the time when Prophet Muhammad, peace and blessings be upon him,

---

[3] Bukhari, *Maghazi*, 36.
[4] Tirmidhi, *Birr*, 51.

was at the height of his power—all the casualties from the wars in which the Prophet participated in the total was about 150 martyrs from the Muslim side, and about 250 people from the enemy's side (Hamidullah 1981, 21). The main factor behind the fact that Islam became a power that drew people by winning their hearts over a period of 10 years and over a vast geography should be sought within the fundamentals of Islamic beliefs and thoughts, and the philosophy of life that it represented, from the intelligence of the Prophet and his being the Prophet of mercy, and from the atmosphere of trust he established.

Conclusion

The principle in Islam is peace. Differences in faith are never a good reason for war. The reasons that make war inevitable always arise due to the violation of some principles. There are certain rules and regulations for taking the life of an enemy, even in wartime. These rules have been established by the Qur'an and the Prophet; these are rules that were meticulously adhered to during the reign of the first caliphs, and which later became the code of the rules of war found in the Islamic law.

According to the law, the permission to kill—no matter what faith a person believes in—is restricted to combatants actively participating in an active war, to combatants who are determined to inflict harm (Merginani 1986, 2/138). Those who do not fulfill these conditions are considered innocent, and their life should be secure. Thus, assaults on civilian targets are not in agreement with the principles of Islam, even during wartime, and this includes suicide attacks. Legitimate goals cannot be reached by illegitimate means.

References

Bilmen, Ö. Nasuhi. *Hukukı İslâmiyye ve Istilahatı Fıkhiyye Kamusu,* Istanbul.

Bukhari, Abu Abdillah Muhammad ibn Ismail. *as-Sahih*, Istanbul.

Bursalı, M. Tahir. *Osmanlı Müellifleri*, Istanbul: 1972.

Abu Yusuf, Yakub ibn Ibrahim. *Kitab al-Haraj*, Beirut: AH 1302 (1910).

Elmalılı, M. Hamdi Yazır. *Hak Dini Kur'an Dili*, Istanbul: 1979.

Hamidullah, Muhammed. *Hazreti Peygamberin Savaşları*, Istanbul: 1981. Originally published as *Battlefields of the Prophet Muhammad.*

——. *Majmu'a al-Wasaik al-Siyasiyya*, Beirut: 1987.

Ibn Hisham. *As-Sirat an-Nabawiyya.*

Kasani, Alauddin Abu Bakr ibn Masud. *Badaiu al-Sanai' fi Tartibi al-Sharai'*, Beirut: 1986.

Merginani, Burhanuddin, *Al-Hidaya Sharhu Bidayat al-Mubtadi*, Istanbul: 1986.

Muslim ibn Hajja. *as-Sahih*, Beirut: 1955.

Semerkandi, Alauddin. *Tuhfat al-Fuqaha*, Beirut: 1984.

Sarahsi, Muhammed ibn Ahmad. *al-Mabsut*, Beirut: 1986.

——. *Sharhu Kitabi's-Seerah al-Kabir*, Beirut: 1997.

Tirmidhi, Muhammad ibn Isa. *al-Jami' al-Sahih*, Beirut.

Waqidi, Muhammad ibn 'Umar ibn Vakıd. *Kitab al-Maghazi*, Oxford: 1966.

Yaman, Ahmet. *İslâm Hukukunda Uluslararası İlişkiler*, Ankara: 1998.

MURDER AND ITS PUNISHMENT IN THE QUR'AN AND THE TORAH

Adil Öksüz

Life is one of the most important values for God, for it is the ultimate blessing, the climax of existence. Life is the origin and the essence of everything; it makes anything associated with it the lord of almost everything else. Any living being can say that "all that exists is my possession; the world is my home; the universe is a gift given to me by my Lord," for it is life which connects us with everything, which allows us to benefit from everything.

Moreover, life—the fruit of the tree of existence—is the crossroads of existence. From this perspective, i.e., that life is the center, or a target at which everything else is directed—life is the brightest proof of the unity of God Almighty, the finest demonstration of His Mercy, and the most complex example of His art. In short, if there were no life, existence would lose its meaning and become undistinguishable from non-existence.

It is because this importance of life, especially the life of human beings—the most perfect form—is not quantitative, but qualitative in nature (in other words it is not divisible by the quantity of people) that one person's life represents the lives of all. It is for this reason that in the Qur'an one person's life is equal to the lives of all human beings, thus, murdering one person is considered to be the same as murdering all humans, and equally, saving the life of one person is regarded as being the same as saving the lives of all people (Ma'ida 5:32). In the context of this assessment, it is recorded (in the Qur'an) that this was also an order that was given to the Israelites, i.e., this is a principle that exists in the Torah.

Murder is regarded as being a major crime and one of the capital sins in both the Qur'an and the Torah. This prohibition is one of the most consistently strict verdicts that exists in all monotheistic religions. If the person who takes the life of another is in contravention of the laws, if the act is intentional and results in death, then the penalty for the perpetrator is death, both in the Qur'an and in the Torah (Baqara 2:178-179; Exodus 21:12; Leviticus 24:17-18).[1]

This action, prohibited by the imperative *You shall not kill!* in the Torah (Exodus 20:13), is also the sixth of the Ten Commandments. This rule protects the fundamental right of a human being's right to life, and emphasizes the importance of the sanctity of human life. In Judaism "to kill" (*qatl*) is defined as "to end someone else's life."[2] Islamic scholars have defined the verb *qatl* as "an act causing the soul to leave the body."[3]

Murder in the Torah and the Establishment of the Crime

The command *You shall not kill*, as recorded in Exodus 20:13, derives from Hebrew root of "*r-ts-h*." This word, as explained by Rashbam and Bekhor Shor, can only be used for "the act of killing unjustly," and thus is not used to describe killings that are part of executions carried out as punishments or deaths that occur during war. It is also not used to describe the cases when the subject of the verb (i.e., the person who commits the act of killing) is God or one of the angels. This prohibition is justified in Genesis 9:6 on the grounds that "if someone sheds blood, his blood needs to be shed by another human, for God created hu-

---

[1] Baruch 1989, 167.
[2] Suzan Alalu *et al.* 2001, p. 156.
[3] Jurjani, *Ta'rifat*, entry "q-t-l," p. 172; Abu al-Baka, *Kulliyyat*, p. 729; Ragib, *Mufradat*, entry "q-t-l"; Bilmen, Vol. III, p. 17.

manity from His own spirit." That means that life, created from God's own spirit, is absolutely sacred, and the right to take it, as well as the right to bestow it, belongs solely to God. Thus, anyone who takes a life usurps this sacred right with this indescribably horrific act, and violates the sovereignty of God. Since humans are created as sacred beings, a killer also denigrates the glory of God. It is for this reason that it is not in the domain of human beings to forgive a killer, or to remove the death penalty and replace it with monetary fines, as explained in Numbers 35:31.[4]

While the Torah declares that those who have been charged with the crime of murder must be sentenced to death, the Verbal Law (the Talmud) sets out some restrictive regulations so as to determine what constitutes this crime. According to the Talmud, the killer must be warned just before committing the crime by two eyewitnesses that the action they are about to carry out is prohibited, and that they will be punished with the death penalty; the killer must declare that they are aware of these facts. In addition, the eyewitnesses must witness the act of murder. Even after all this, no matter how strong the evidence is, it is not enough by itself to establish that the crime had been committed. The case has to be brought before a religious court that consists of 23 judges. While a simple majority, with a margin of one vote, is enough for acquittal, for a guilty verdict to be passed the majority must be two votes. However, even if the judges convict the criminal unanimously, this punishment will be difficult to be carried out. R. Akiva and R. Tarfon remind that they had served in a court that was concerned with such crimes, and that no one had ever been sentenced to death. Despite the fact that the courts usually do not inflict the death penalty, those who are found

---

[4] Nahum M. Sarna, *Bible Commentary: Exodus*, Philadelphia: The JPS (Jewish Publication Society), 1991, 20/13, p. 113.

guilty are sentenced to a long term of imprisonment.[5] In modern Israel, there is no death penalty for the crime of murder.[6]

Murder and Its Penalty in the Torah

The Torah, like the Qur'an, differentiates between the crime and the penalty for murder in terms of whether the act was intentional or accidental, relating this to the penal law. According to the Torah, the penalty for the intentional taking of a life is the death sentence (Exodus 21:12, 14, 23-25; Leviticus 24:17-18; Numbers 35:16-21; Deuteronomy 19:11, 21). Renowned scholars of the Torah provide detailed information in the context of the commentaries of the verses that are related to these penal codes. For instance, according to the famous commentator Maimonides, whoever intentionally kills a man violates one of the "Ten Commandments" (Exodus 20:13; 21:20), and should be condemned to death. If the killer commits the crime with any metal object or with fire then the death sentence is execution by decapitation with a sword.[7]

Also according to another prominent commentator of the Torah, Hirsh, life is a value in and of itself, superior to all other things; it is the basic phenomena connecting all that is on the Earth. The following statements illustrate this point:

> He that smites a man, so that he dies, shall be surely put to death. And if a man lie not in wait, but God deliver (him) into his hand; then I will appoint him a place whither he shall flee. (Exodus 21:12-13)

> And he that kills any man shall surely be put to death. (Leviticus 24:17)

---

[5] Besalel, Yusuf. *Yahudilik Ansiklopedisi*, II, 317.
[6] Ibid. II, 318.
[7] Moses Maimonides. *Code of Maimonides, Book Eleven, the Book of Torts,* Yale University Press: 1954. Translated from Hebrew into English by Hyman Klein. pp. 195-203.

In these verses, only the men seem to be mentioned as the victims of the crime. Talmudic scholars say that the killing of women and children are not within the scope of *qatl*. The act of killing is associated with the act of "smiting" if the intention of this act was to kill. Moreover, the "smiting" and the "death" as a consequence of this action have been isolated to clarify the idea of intention in the crime. The death penalty here is incumbent upon the intentional taking of life. Penalties for manslaughter (unintentional death) are explained in other verses of the Torah. Despite the fact that Hirsh describes life as being the most fundamental value, he argues—in the context of the commentaries of these verses where the value of life is discussed—that in cases where the deceased is a woman or a child, then these verses do not apply; the penalty for such cases are not the subjects of these verses. This shows that to some commentators of the Torah, the life of an adult male is evaluated differently than that of a woman or a child.[8]

However, the well-known commentator Rashi (1040-1105) when commenting on the same verses argues that the wording differentiates a "man" and "any person" in these verses. He points out that "If we take these two verses together, it is obvious that the emphasis is (not on who the killer is, but) on the way the killer strikes, and the intention involved." Rashi adopts the view that even if the victim does not die after being struck with an intention to kill, the perpetrator will still be charged for murder, and will be given the death sentence. The death sentence which the verse stipulates as being applicable when "a man who strikes a person and kills him," is only valid if the blow is fatal. And according to Rashi, this verse does not differentiate between a male, female, or immature victim; thus whether the person actually killed or intended to be killed is a man, or a woman, or a child,[9] the perpetrator will be sentenced to death. The other

---

[8] Hirsh, II, 304.
[9] At this point, a discussion on the case of a fetus takes place. According to the Torah, a baby born 2 months premature (i.e., when it is a 7 month old fetus) does live; whereas a

verses of the Torah that are related to intentional murder and the penal laws that pertain to it and commentaries of the scholars of Judaism are as follows:

> But if a man come presumptuously upon his neighbor, to slay
> him with guile; you shall take him from mine altar, that he may
> die. (Exodus 21:14)

Rashi clarifies some of the ambiguities in this verse. According to him, the following do not count as intentional death: to kill an infidel; the death of a patient under treatment by a doctor; the death of a convict during the execution of the "sentence of 40 whips" in the hands of the officers of the court; the death of a child while being punished by his father; the death of a pupil being disciplined by the teacher; or the death of a person caused by a stone that was thrown to kill somebody else. All these "causes of death" are separated from other deaths that have been intentionally committed by guile or treachery. Those who kill a man by the use of guile will be killed; even if the murderer were a rabbi in his synagogue, he will be taken from the altar of God and executed.

According to some other commentators, the word "a man" in verses 24:17-18 of the Leviticus, denotes any person, including women and children. The usage of the phrase "soul for soul" at the end of the verse to include animals is interpreted as being the monetary value of any animal killed, with compensation being paid to the owner.[10] In the same vein, it is concluded from the clause "whoever kills a person, the penalty for the perpetrator is the death sentence," that the verdict is still applicable for cases where the killer is a woman or a child.[11]

---

baby born 1 month premature (that is 8 month old fetus) does not. Thus, slaughtering the latter is out of the scope of this penalty. (Rashi, II, 304; Rosenberg and Cohen 1947, 474).
[10] Rosenberg and Cohen 1947, 760.
[11] Rashi, III, 112a-113.

And he that kills a beast, he shall restore it: and he that kills a
man, he shall be put to death. You shall have one manner of
law, as well for the stranger, as for one of your own country: for
I (am) the Lord your God. (Leviticus 24:21-22)

The above decisively shows the distinction between humans
and animals in the Torah. The law of the Torah regards human
beings as "people," but animals as "possessions." Thus, the death
sentence is incumbent upon a crime committed against human
beings. At the end of the verse, the equality of the right of life for
everybody, stranger or neighbor is focused on.[12]

The phrase *he who kills an animal* in the aforementioned
verse indicates inflicting fatal harm that ends in the animal's
death.[13] Likewise, those who injure a human fatally and cause
him or her to die will be sentenced to similar penalties. However,
in the case of harm done to one's own parents, the harm itself
will be regarded as being the same as if death had been the result.
Even if the parent does not die of the injuries suffered at the
moment of attack, the child who injured the parent fatally will
still be sentenced to death.[14]

And if he smites him with an instrument of iron, so that he dies,
he (is) a murderer: the murderer shall surely be put to death.
And if he smites him with throwing a stone, wherewith he may
die, and he dies, he (is) a murderer: the murderer shall surely be
put to death. Or (if) he smites him with a hand weapon of wood,
wherewith he may die, and he dies, he (is) a murderer: the murderer shall surely be put to death. The revenger of blood himself
shall slay the murderer: when he meets him, he shall slay him.
But if he thrusts him of hatred, or hurls at him by laying of wait,
that he dies; or in enmity smites him with his hand, that he dies:
he that smote (him) shall surely be put to death; (for) he (is) a

---

[12] Hirschler, p. 486-487.
[13] Rosenberg and Cohen 1947, 760; Rashi, III, 112b.
[14] Rashi, III, 112b.

murderer: the revenger of blood shall slay the murderer, when he meets him. (Numbers 35:16-21)

These verses are concerned with the act of murder and the criteria used to establish the offence. For instance, the general information given about the act of murder, and the tools utilized, the evidence and the conditions are all subject matter of these verses. The text provides the basis for court hearings; especially Numbers 35:16, where the size of the weapon, what it is made of, its features, the strength of power the user (i.e., the killer) expended when using it, the physical condition of the victim, and the wounds inflicted upon him, are all detailed.[15] In this verse, the penalty for the intentional killing of another person is emphasized by the phrase "for he is a murderer, and shall be put to death."[16] Priority is given to metal (used as a weapon) because sometimes a small piece of metal can cause more damage than a large piece of wood; if the injury is fatal, then the assaulter is condemned to death.[17] The priority here is on the lethality of the weapon and on the intention of the one who wields the weapon.

The subject matter in Numbers 35:17-19 turns to stone and wood, which do not cause fatal injuries when wielded in normal conditions and sizes, but which may inflict fatal injuries if they are larger.[18] At the end of the verse, a tool made of stone or wood for the purpose of hitting and killing is specified. It is emphasized in the two verses that the tool or weapon used to hit a man should be of a size capable of killing. The penalty for those who use such a tool or weapon for the purpose of killing is without question the death sentence. Even if the killer takes refuge in a sanctuary, such as a synagogue, they will not be able to escape execution, as those from the immediate family of the victim has the right to kill them wherever they are found.[19]

---

[15] Hirschler, p. 643.
[16] Rosenberg and Cohen 1947, 979.
[17] Hirsh, IV, 559.
[18] Rosenberg and Cohen 1947, 980.
[19] Rashi, IV, 168

According to these verses of the Torah discussed here, if the perpetrator is found guilty of the crime, and the relatives of the victim are present at the court hearing, then the court turns the criminal over to them. If the court refuses to give the accused over to the relatives of the victim after the guilty verdict has been passed, or if the victim escapes, the relatives of the victim maintain their right for execution wherever they can find the murderer.[20] In short, the Torah, in some sense, accepts the right of an individual to carry out an execution.

Another phrase that defines intention in the act of murder, and which incurs the death penalty, is phrased as *if he thrusts him of hatred* in verse 35:20 of Numbers. According to the commentator of the Torah, Chumash, the phrase *if he thrusts* means "to push from a high place to make him fall."[21] When using a weapon or tool to kill a person the intention is clear; it is for this reason that such acts are prioritized in verses 16-18 of Numbers. Subsequently, other acts that result in death are listed. In fact, whatever method is employed, the intention in the mind is the same, and thus the penalty given is the same. The verse *Moreover you shall take no satisfaction for the life of a murderer, which (is) guilty of death: but he shall be surely put to death* (Numbers 35:31) ensures that the penalty for "intentional killing" is the death penalty, with no other alternative. With this verse, any other alternatives, such as the payment of compensation, have clearly been eliminated.[22]

The verdict commonly known as *qisas* (the law of retaliation) exists in the Torah as well. For instance:

> And if (any) mischief follow, then you shall give life for life,
> eye for eye, tooth for tooth, hand for hand, foot for foot, burning

---

[20] Hirsh, IV, 559.
[21] Rosenberg and Cohen 1947, 980.
[22] Jacob Milgrom, *Bible Commentary Series: Numbers*, Philadelphia: The JPS (Jewish Publication Society), 1991. Verses 35:30-31, p. 295.

140 *Terror and Suicide Attacks: An Islamic Perspective*

for burning, wound for wound, stripe for stripe. (Exodus 21:23-25)

And your eye shall not pity; (but) life (shall go) for life, eye for eye, tooth for tooth, hand for hand, foot for foot. (Deuteronomy 19:21)

Breach for breach, eye for eye, tooth for tooth: as he hath caused a blemish in a man, so shall it be done to him (again). (Leviticus 24:20)

The Issue of *Qatl* in the Qur'an

There are many verses in the Qur'an that forbid killing. God Almighty commands (with regard to this meaning) in chapter Isra:

Take not life which God has made sacred, except for just cause. And if anyone is slain wrongfully, we have given his heir authority (to demand *qisas* or to forgive): but let him not exceed bounds in the matter of taking life: for he is helped (by the Law). (Isra 17:33)

In another verse, the Qur'an declares that killing without a just cause is regarded as a crime committed against all humanity:

. . . whoever kills a soul, unless it be for manslaughter or for mischief in the land, is like one who killed the whole of mankind (Ma'ida 5:32)[23]

---

[23] For similar expressions in Talmud see Mawdudi, *Tafhim*, I/495: "Whoever murders, takes a life of Israel, from the stand point of the Book of God, he destroys the whole world. And who protects a life of Israel, he saves the whole world in the sight of the Book of God." Moreover, it is recorded in the Talmud that the judges of the Israelites used to address the witnesses by saying "whoever takes a man's life, he should be interrogated as if he had killed all the people of the world."

There are also verses where it is declared that crimes will not go unpunished, and the perpetrators will be penalized accordingly (Baqara 2:178-179; Ma'ida, 5:45).

In Islam, the unlawful killing of a person is regarded as a crime, and it is one of the major sins. This offense is listed among the seven major sins by the Prophet that sentence their perpetrators to the sufferings of this world and hereafter, i.e., that demand *qisas* in this world, and the punishment of eternal hell-fire in the next.[24] The taking of human life is a violation against the servants of God, whom He has made sacred, and against life; it is a threat to public security and to the fabric of society.

The term *qatl* means "to kill somebody; to deprive a living being of life." It is defined as "the causative action of taking the soul out of body."[25] Those people who kill another living being cause the soul to leave the body, and these people are known as murderers, while the one who has been killed is called the victim.[26] According to Islam, taking the life of another unjustly is one of the greatest offenses, second only to *shirk* (associating partners with God).[27] God is the one who gives life, thus without His permission, or without considering the regulations He has set, no one can take it away. Every single person's life is sacred, inviolable, and protected, except in cases where the death penalty is deserved and has been decided on by a legal authority. Any punishment that has been decided on can only be carried out by a legally appointed body. And even the death penalty, which permits the taking of a human life, is also restricted by certain regulations. The Prophet, peace and blessings be upon him, declared that killing a Muslim, who bears witness that there is no deity but God, and that Muhammad is His messenger, can only be permissible under the following three situations: either as a retaliation for a life that has been taken; or as a punishment for adultery by

---

[24] Bukhari, *Hudud*, 44; Muslim, *Iman*, 144-145.
[25] Jurjani, *Ta'rifat*, p. 172; Abu al-Baka, *Kulliyyat*, p. 729; Ragib, *Mufradat*, "q-t-l"; Zuhayli, *Fiqh al-Islami*, VI, 217.
[26] Bilmen, Ömer Nasuhi, *Hukuk-u İslamiyye*, III, 17.
[27] Muslim, *Iman*, 144; Bukhari, *Hudud*, 44.

married people, or as a punishment for apostatizing from Islam, and not being repentant within the given period, which is the penalty for violation of the previously adopted contract.[28]

There are many hadiths relating to the subject some of which are as follows: "Killing a Muslim unjustly is as great an offense as exterminating the whole world."[29] "If all the people of Heaven and Earth came together, and joined in killing one Muslim, God would certainly throw them into hellfire face first, making them all low and contemptible."[30] "There is no doubt that your blood and your possessions are inviolable to you."[31]

In another hadith, the Prophet warned of "Seven destructive things"; among these "taking a life, which God has made sacred, except for a just cause"[32] is also listed. Another hadith cautions that "those who kill a non-Muslim who has made an agreement with Muslims; or a non-Muslim subject who has accepted Islamic authority, will not even come close to Paradise."[33]

Islamic scholars have made different categorizations of the types of killing. According to the Hanafi school there are five categories: Intentional killing, quasi-intentional killing, accidental killing, quasi-accidental killing, and killing by means of another.[34] According to the overwhelming majority of scholars (literally known as the *jumhur*—including the Hanbali and Shafii scholars—the number of categories is three, and according to Maliki scholars it is two. Here, we will follow the categorization in three types, namely, intentional killing; quasi-intentional killing; and accidental killing.

---

[28] Bukhari, *Diyat*, 6; Muslim, *Kasame*, 25-26.

[29] Nasai, *Tahrim ad-Dam*, 2.

[30] Tirmidhi, *Diyat*, 8.

[31] Bukhari, *Ilm*, 37; Muslim, *Hajj*, 147.

[32] Bukhari, *Hudud*, 44; Müslim, *Iman*, 144-145.

[33] Bukhari, *Diyat* 30; Abu Dawud, *Jihad* 153.

[34] Udah, Abdulkadir. *Al-Tashri al-Jinaiyy al-Islami*, II, 8-9, Beirut: Muassasa al-Risale, 1996; Zuhayli, *Fiqh al-Islami*, VI, 221.

Murder and Its Penalty in the Qur'an

After having established that the taking of a life is a religiously forbidden offense, the Qur'an goes on to establish the penalty as the retaliation, if the heirs of the victim are not content with a ransom in this world although *remitting retaliation by way of charity* is encouraged (Baqara 2:178; Ma'ida 5:45), and eternal hellfire—if God does not pardon—in the Hereafter (Nisa 4:93; Zumar 39:53). In fact, for those who believe, the punishment of the Hereafter is the real penalty, indeed, the greatest, and the harshest penalty. That is to say, that being condemned to a punishment in the realm of eternity because of taking someone's life is a penalty whose horror makes a believer tremble with fear and prevents him or her from even daring to think of such an action. From this perspective, the penalties relating to the Hereafter constitute a strong ethical sanction. That is why God Almighty commands:

> If a man kills a believer intentionally his recompense is Hell to abide therein forever: and the wrath and the curse of God are upon him and a dreadful penalty is prepared for him. (Nisa 4:93)

There is no other offense in the Qur'an that has such a harsh threat connected with it.

The most comprehensive verse in the Qur'an on the laws related to the offense of taking a life and the penalty connected is the following one found in chapter Baqara:

> O you who believe! Retaliation is prescribed for you in the matter of the slain, the free for the free, and the slave for the slave, and the female for the female, but if any remission is made by the brother of the slain, then (the killing for retaliation is annulled) grant any reasonable demand and compensate him with handsome gratitude. This is a concession and a Mercy from you

> Lord; so whoever exceeds the limit after this he shall have a
> painful chastisement. (Baqara 2:178)

This verse determines that retaliation or *qisas* is a requirement which can only be overcome if one of the heirs of the slain
forgives—and that this (i.e., forgiveness) is the better and more
favorable approach. It is permissible to agree upon a certain
value in lieu of retaliation. This verse declares the equality of all
with respect to "right to life." It modifies the Judaic Law in terms
of its jurisdiction that forgiveness is unacceptable and the Christian ruling in which killing in retaliation is not allowed; it
stresses the priority of ransom over retaliation and puts an end to
the Arab traditions and laws which allow the taking of human
life in the name of honor, violating human rights and disregard-
ing the equality of right to life.[35] According to Muslim scholars,
in the original text of the Torah, forgiveness and ransom did not
exist; there was only a death penalty.[36] In fact, the Prophet, peace
and blessings be upon him, said that "For the Children of Israel,
there was no ransom, there was only retaliation."[37] This hadith is
supported by the following verse found in the Torah of today:

> You will not accept ransom for the soul of the killer who de-
> served death; he shall certainly be killed. (Numbers 35:31)

According to the Torah, it is not possible to escape death by
paying a ransom.[38]

Forgiveness and Ransom

Islam, as a code of law, permits person retaliation after having
been wronged; justice requires mutuality in protection of inviola-

---

[35] Yazır, Elmalılı M. Hamdi. *Hak Dini Kur'an Dili*, 1/601.
[36] Zamahshari, *Kashshaf*, al-Baqara, 178, I, 220; Radhi, *Mafatih*, al-Baqara, 178, II, 221,
225.
[37] Bukhari, *Tafsir*, 23, Diyat, 8.
[38] Rashi, IV, 170.

ble values (Baqara 2:94). Nevertheless, retaliation for a wrong by doing something equal is not demanded. In many verses of the Qur'an, people are encouraged to forgive the wrong doings that they have suffered, as this is the more virtuous behavior. For instance:

> Do not forget generosity and liberality between yourselves. For God sees well all that you do. (Baqara 2:237)

> Nor can goodness and evil be equal. Repel (evil) with what is better! (Fussilat 41:34)

> Do not forget that the recompense for an injury is an injury equal thereto (in degree): but if a person forgives and makes reconciliation his reward is due from God: for God loves not those who do wrong. (Shura 42:40)

> But indeed if any shows patience and forgives, that would truly be an exercise of courageous, will, and resolution in the conduct of affairs. (Shura 42:43)

Islam also warns that when executing a punishment as retaliation for an offense, the boundaries should not be exceeded (Isra 17:33).

Here we should note that individuals should be encouraged to forgive the wrong doings they have suffered. However, individuals do not have the authority to forgive the violations committed against society, the sacred values, or the values that God has put forth. As society and government cannot forgive an assault on behalf of the individual, nor can the individual exercise the power of forgiveness on behalf of society. The Qur'an also warns society with regard to the execution of the penalties and advises the maintenance of the limits of piety:

> If anyone transgresses the prohibition against you (your values),
> transgress you likewise (without exceeding) against him. But
> fear God and restrain, and know that God is with those who re-
> strain themselves. (Baqara 2:194)

The Qur'an points out an important matter concerning the penalty inflicted on the killer which is not mentioned in the Torah: the right of preference and forgiveness given to the heirs of the slain, as the following verse states *But if any remission is made by the brother of the slain, then (the killing for retaliation is annulled) grant any reasonable demand and compensate him with handsome gratitude. This is a concession and a Mercy from you Lord* (Baqara 2:178). There is consolation here for the killer; forgiveness of the punishment is possible. There is also consolation here for the family of the victim; the acceptance of compensation is permissible. And having these three options (retaliation, forgiveness, and compensation) is a comfort and a mercy bestowed upon Muslim society by God.[39] This kindness is a gift that requires the gratitude of Muslims. It is a legal remedy given to Muslims in order to allow people to continue on living their lives by establishing reconciliation, without the taking of yet another life.[40] In fact, the Prophet, peace and blessings be upon him, clarified this issue by saying the following:

> Whoever is killed, even unjustly, his heirs have the option to
> choose one of the following three options: either retaliation, or
> forgiveness, or compensation. If he chooses a fourth alternative
> then hold his hand (restrain him).[41]

If the murderer's family gives a certain amount of money or goods to the victim's family, the retaliation is immediately annulled before the court hearing, provided that both sides have

---

[39] Alusi, *Ruh al-Maani*, Baqara, 178, I, 51.
[40] Qutb, *Fi zilal al Qur'an*, Baqara, 178, I, 164.
[41] Abu Dawud, *Diyat*, 3, 4; Tirmidhi, *Diyat*, 13.

agreed upon this arrangement beforehand. Then both sides are obliged to comply with the conditions prescribed in the tradition; i.e., the family of the victim is expected to show mercy and forgiveness, whereas the murderer has to pay traditionally accepted amount of ransom to the other side.[42] If the murderer has been forgiven without any preconditioned amount in terms of ransom, then the victim's family should abide with this favor, and should not demand anything from then on.[43] Since partial retaliation is not possible, forgiveness is absolute, even though it may be partial.[44] Similarly, if an elderly from the family of the victim forgives the murderer, it is regarded as an absolute forgiveness by the entire family.

Deprivation from Birthright and Inheritance

Outside the abovementioned rulings in Islam, there is another ruling maintained in the Prophet's sunna, which prohibits a murderer's being an heir to the victim. It has been widely acknowledged by scholars that murder as a crime constitutes obstacle for rights related with inheritance and birthright. The Prophet is reported to have said the following on this issue: "There is no will for any murderer."[45] In another report he said, "A murderer can not receive anything as inheritance."[46] Thus, if an heir or any person who has a right on the will kills the predecessor, they will be deprived from the inheritance and the will. Hanafi jurists stipulate that the crime should be committed by the murder himself (*mubasharat*) rather than indirect and unintentional involvement (*tasabbub*) in someone's death. In *mubasharat*, it does not make any difference whether murder took place intentionally or through an accident.

---

[42] Jassas, *Ahkam*, I, 184.
[43] Ibn Humam, X, 239.
[44] Yazır, Bakara, 178, I, 604-605. See Radhi, *Mafatih*, Bakara, 178, II, 225-6.
[45] Ibn Maja, *Diyat*, 14; Ahmad ibn Hanbal, *Musnad*, 1/49.
[46] Zaylai, *Nasb ar-Raya*, 4/402.

References

Baruch A. Levine. *Bible Commentary Series: Leviticus,* Philadelphia: The JPS (Jewish Publication Society): 1989.

Suzan Alalu *et al.* Sara Yanarocak, *Yahudilikte Kavram ve Değerler,* Istanbul: 2001, Gözlem Gazetecilik Basın ve Yayın A.Ş.

Bilmen, Ömer Nasuhi, *Hukukı İslâmiyye ve Istılahatı Fıkhıyye Kamusu,* Istanbul: Bilmen Basım ve Yayınevi.

Nahum M. Sarna, *Bible Commentary Series: Exodus,* Philadelphia: The JPS (Jewish Publication Society): 1991.

Yusuf Besalel, *Yahudilik Ansiklopedisi,* II, 317.

Moses Maimonides. *Code of Maimonides, Book Eleven, the Book of Torts,* Yale University Press: 1954. Translated from Hebrew into English by Hyman Klein.

Rashi (Rabbi Solomon ben Isaac or Shlomo Yitzhaki).

Rosenberg, A. J., A. Cohen. *Soncino Chumash,* England: 1947.

Hirschler, Gertrude. *Ashkenaz: The German Jewish Heritage,* New York: Yeshiva University Museum, 1988.

Hirsh, Rav Samson Raphael, *Commentary on Genesis 22:2,* New York: Judaica Press, 1971.

Jacob Milgrom, *Bible Commentary Series: Numbers,* Philadelphia: The JPS (Jewish Publication Society): 1991.

Mawdudi, *Tafhim.*

Udeh, Abdulkadir, *At-Tashri al-Jinai al-Islami,* Beirut: Muassasa al-Risala, 1996.

Yazır, Elmalılı M. Hamdi, *Hak Dini Kur'an Dili.*

Kasani, Alauddin Abu Bakr Ibn Masud. *Badaiu's-Sanai' fî Tartibi ash-Sharai',* VII, 351-352, Beirut: Dar al- Fiqr, 1996.

Az-Zuhayli, *Fıqh al-Islami.*

Jassas, *Ahkam.*

Kurtubî, *Ahkam,* Nisa.

Alusi, *Ruhu'l-Maani,* Baqara.

Qutb, *Fi Zilal al-Qur'an,* Baqara, 178, I, 164.

Jabr Mahmud al-Fudaylat, *Sukut al-Ukubat fi'l-Fıqhi al-Islami*. Edited by Ahmad (Halifa), Amman: Dar al-Ammar, 1987.

Ibn Humam, *Fath al-Qadir*.

INDEX

INDEX